DANIEL O'DONNELL'S IRELAND

Songs and Scenes from My Homeland

THE OFFICIAL ILLUSTRATED BOOK
DANIEL O'DONNELL AND MICHAEL J McDONAGH

First published in Great Britain in 2007 by Virgin Books Ltd
Thames Wharf Studios, Rainville Road, London W6 9HA

A catalogue record for this book is available from the British Library.

ISBN 978 1 9052 6408 7

The paper used in this book is a natural, recyclable product made from wood grown in sustainable forests. The manufacturing process conforms to the regulations of the country of origin.

Printed and bound in Germany

ART DIRECTION & DESIGN
Dave Richardson & Julia Kennedy / TIGERRIFIC

PRINCIPLE PHOTOGRAPHY
Michael J McDonagh

CONSULTANT EDITOR
Eddie Rowley

ADDITIONAL PHOTOGRAPHY
Barry McCall, Mike Smallcombe, Daniel Ward, Kip Carrol

SPECIAL THANKS TO
I am most grateful to my family, my management and my record company and to all my fans who have given to me so much support. To Mick McDonagh, Eddie Rowley, Sean Reilly, Dave Richardson, Julia Kennedy, Carolyn Thorne and everyone at my publishers for all their hard work in making this book possible.

Also a very special thanks must go to songwriter Johnny McCauley who has given to me so many songs included here.

WITH THANKS TO
Denis Allen, John Baird, C Ball, Mary Buckley Clarke, Eithene & Larry Carey, P Cavenagh, Ann Clerkin, Phil Colclough, Joe Collum, J Copeland, Phil Coulter, Gerry Crowley, John Duggan, The Farrelly Family, The Cash Family, The McBride Family, John Farry, Lorreta Flynn, Ian Fussey, Ian McGarry, Sile Gillespie, Brendan Graham, Isla Grant, Mary & Maurice Harnett, Frank Hennessy, D Henry, Mark & Jane Hewlett, Pete St John, Metta & Jessica Kreissig, Mrs Thomas Long, Peter & Jane Mantle, Colohon McCullough, Chris McDonagh, Mr & Mrs George McLoughlin, Jim & Kate Nicholson, K North, Denis O'Brien, Julia O'Donnell, Majella O'Donnell, Roderick & Helena Perceval, Simon Platz, A Quinn, Mark Helmore, Aly Raftery, Andy Reynolds, Marc Roberts, Lou Robin, M Sage, Rita Skerrit, David Smith, Alex Towers, Denis Vaughan, Sheena White, Omagh District Council

Brook Lane Hotel, Clonalis House, Coolclogher House, Danny Minnies, Herbert Park Hotel, Delphi Lodge, Glanleam House, Glenbeigh House, Kerry Bog Village, Kilmokea House, Lismacue House, Martinstown House, Mount Vernon, Temple Mount, The Slieve Donard Hotel, Ulster Folk & Transport Museum, Mount Stewart

Bourne Music, Carlin Music, Emma Music, Four Seasons Music, Four Roads Music, Green Grass Music, McCullough Piggot, Misty River Music, New Moon Music, Peter Maurice Music, Rosette Records, Rosette Music, Valentine Music, Velvet Music, Walton's

Every effort has been made to credit and trace the songwriters and copyright holders of the lyrics included in this book and I am very grateful to all of you for providing me with so many wonderful songs to sing. I also appreciate the hospitality shown by the owners of homes and gardens and hotels throughout Ireland when the pictures were being taken. If inadvertently, any name or permission has been overlooked, I apologise and hope you approve of their inclusion here.

Canon Cameras, Stenna Line Ferries

OFFICIAL WEBSITE: www.danielodonnell.org

CONTENTS

INTRODUCTION

Wherever I travel, and in my business I am lucky to travel more than most to so many fantastic places, my heart always lies at home. Home for me is and always will be the special place in IRELAND where I grew up, Donegal.

Donegal is the county at the top of the country to the north west of the island. It is remote, rugged and beautiful with much of the county facing the sea. I grew up here learning songs and stories with my family in our kitchen, in the small village of Kincasslagh. These modest beginnings made me who I am and have allowed me to travel the world proud of my Irish heritage and my roots.

Donegal is just a small part of our wonderful country and this book is my chance to share with you some of my favourite songs and scenes from our enchanted green island.

Daniel xx

ABOUT THE BOOK

The career of Daniel O'Donnell has been remarkable. From humble beginnings in a remote part of Ireland, years before the Celtic Tiger had transformed the country, Daniel went on to pack out concert venues all over the English-speaking world. He has sold millions of albums and DVDs and captivates audiences wherever he plays. The first unique ingredient to Daniel's success is the 'what you see is what you get' honest charm of Daniel himself, who communicates with all his fans as if they are personal friends joining him at home for a sing-along session. There is nothing manufactured about Daniel, in an age when celebrity success is created overnight. Natural talent, integrity and old-fashioned values of respect, concern for others and a great sense of humour are ingrained in Daniel from his upbringing in Ireland. This is what makes his career enduring as he goes on to win more and more fans and the respect of his peers.

In 2004 Daniel O'Donnell collaborated with Mick McDonagh, his long-time creative consultant, and Eddie Rowley on a bestselling illustrated book, *My Pictures & Places*, to give to his fans a fascinating behind-the-scenes look at the pictures, photos sessions, locations and video shoots that Daniel and Mick had worked on together for over 25 years.

A key ingredient to Daniel's success is his choice of music, so much of it Irish in origin. Daniel came from a musical family, his elder sister, Margaret, paving the way as an Irish singing star before Daniel started out. In the days before television, computers and downloads, he grew up learning songs from his family and friends and when he commenced his own career he became something of a rebel for his generation by singing material that was not fashionable amongst his peers. Daniel only sang the songs that he wanted to sing, with no compromise.

In this follow-up illustrated book, Daniel relates the stories behind his favourite songs and through original landscape pictures taken specially by Mick, reveals some of the places in Ireland associated with many of them.

Cead Mille Failte...
A Hundred Thousand Welcomes is the traditional greeting for visitors to Ireland but sometimes it can be a bit confusing. Thousands of visitors arrive daily at Dun Laogharie on the car ferries but they have to have very quick reactions with only four seconds to decide from this profusion of choice at the first set of lights they come to.

MY HOMELAND

Sure, you all know by now that I come from Kincasslagh, a small village in Donegal. When I grew up here, it was at a time when the world seemed to revolve at a much slower pace, when many of the older traditions were still part of the lifestyle of Ireland. Compared to the boom years we have enjoyed recently, our country was poor and so life was tough for the people. Sadly, so many had to leave their homeland to find work, including my father. But it is a tribute to their love that my childhood memories are happy ones. When my father died when I was a child of six, the tragic and early loss of the head of the family cast a huge shadow over all our lives. My mother, whilst grieving herself, was a tower of strength for us all and a huge source of love and comfort, by working hard to let our lives carry on in a loving home. Our first home was the old house near the sea opposite a new house, where my mother now lives. It was traditional in style at the time, with life centred around the fireside. We moved across the road in 1967 to this new house, which had running hot and cold water and a flush toilet with a bathroom. I am rooted in this small village on the coast of Ireland, under the shadow of Errigal Mountain. That was, and still is, my homeland. Kincasslagh, County Donegal, Ireland.

"My mother's treasured memories of her life and times growing up on the little island of Owey inspired her to pen a beautiful poem, 'My Lovely Island Home'.

Owey Island, situated off the coast of Donegal, was also my island playground as a child. I spent lots of summers there with my grandmother, my uncle, his wife and their family in the home that my mother was brought up in.

Island life was a world apart from the lifestyle of the people on the mainland, even though it was only about a mile off the coast. The islanders seemed to be a very content people. I always felt that there was no urgency to do the daily work, although everything got done. They were very self-sufficient. Obviously fish was the main diet and they grew their own potatoes and baked their own bread. They really lived organically, before being organic was fashionable.

In the 1950s, '60s and '70s, many of the young people from Owey emigrated in search of work. By the 1970s the island still did not have electricity, running water, bathrooms or television. As none of this was available on the island the remaining people decided to make their life on the mainland. I suppose the young people saw the ease of living with all of these modern conveniences. So eventually there was no hope for island life to survive and by the mid '70s the remaining three families left for good.

MY MOTHER JULIA

So, on this last day of Owey being inhabited, my mother was very sad. She realised that nothing had ever been recorded about how they lived their lives there and she knew that night would be the first time that there would be no welcome light in the cottage windows or, as she put it, 'no step' on the island she loved. So she sat down and wrote the poem 'My Lovely Island Home' about Owey.

In 2006, when I was working on an album of my own songs, I put some music to it and was delighted to include it on my CD 'Until The Next Time'. So this song has great significance to me and to our family and to people from Owey Island."

MY LOVELY ISLAND HOME

Daniel O'Donnell / Julia O'Donnell

As I sit here sadly thinking how the years go swiftly past
My thoughts go back to my childhood days when I was but a lad
And we a happy family gathered round our turf fire bright
And the fairytales our parents told on the cold dark wintry nights

My brothers they are married now with families of their own
My sister lives in the USA in her grand Long Island home
She pays a visit now and then to greet us one and all
Then our thoughts go back to those happy times in our
home in Donegal

My island home, where I was born
Oh how I miss those days long gone
The little burn where I would play
Oh how I long for yesterday
If I could return I'd never more roam
Forever to stay in my old island home

My island home lies empty now; the clock hangs on the wall
The fireside chair it still sits there, there's a padlock on the door
The raging seas and the wintry winds and the seagulls wearily cry
But no fire burns bright in our hearth tonight
As it did in days gone by

So fare thee well my island home, where I spent many happy days
And fare thee well to my friends so dear, who have crossed the ocean waves
May God protect and guide you all, wherever you may roam
For Owey was like heaven to us in our lovely island home

My island home, where I was born
Oh how I miss those days long gone
The little burn where I would play
Oh how I long for yesterday
If I could return I'd never more roam
Forever to stay in my old island home

JAMES & MARGARET McGONAGLE
MATERNAL GRANDPARENTS

OWEY ISLAND

CUTTING THE CORN AT CRESSLOUGH (THE EMIGRANT'S LETTER)

Percy French

Dear Danny I'm taking the pen in me hand
To tell you we're just out of sight of the land
In a big anchor liner we're sailing in style
And we're sailing away from the Emerald Isle
Oh a strange sort of sigh seems to come from us all
As the waves hit the last bit of old Donegal
Sure it's good to be you that is taking your tea
Where they are cutting the corn around Cresslough the day

Sure I spoke to the captain and he won't turn around
And if I swum back I'd be out to be drowned
So I'll stay where I am for the diet is great
And there's lots of combustibles piled on me plate
Although it is sumptuous sure I'd swop the whole lot
For the old wooden spoon and the stireabout pot
Oh and Katey foreninst me a-wettin' the tea
Where they are cutting the corn around Cresslough the day

There is a woman on board that knows Katey by sight
And we talked of old times 'til they put out the lights
I'm to meet the good woman tomorrow on deck
And we'll talk about Katey from here to Quebec
Sure I know I'm no match for her, no not the least
With her house and two cows and her brother a priest
But the woman declares Katey's heart's on the sea
Whilst mine's with the reapers round Cresslough the day

Ah goodbye to you Danny there's no more to be said
For I think the salt waters got into me head
And it drips from me eyes when I call to me mind
The friends and the colleens I'm leaving left behind
And sure Katey herself when she bade me goodbye
Had just the slight trace of a tear in her eye
And a break in her voice when she said you might stay
But please God I'll come back to old Cresslough some day

"I recorded this song because it was sung, along with many other people, by Bridie Galagher, who was a singer from Donegal. I always think that Bridie paved the way for all Donegal singers that came after her. I loved the song: I love the tongue-in-cheek approach of Percy French, which is apparent in pretty much all his songs, but especially this one. It's written in the local language. Instead of 'today' it says 'the day': Cutting the Corn around Cresslough 'the day'. The way we would say it at home. It's just such a beautiful, beautiful ballad."

CUTTING THE CORN NEAR THE ROCK OF DUNAMASE, COUNTY LAOISE

DESTINATION DONEGAL

Johnny McCauley

As I stand above the starboard bow and watch the ocean foam
As I view each new horizon I grow further from my home
I'm sailing on a foreign ship that's bound for Montreal
But I'll view the world and make my destination Donegal

I would make my way from Malin to Bundoran through Raphoe
Or Portsalon down to Killybegs by Cresslough and Dungloe
I'd wander round by Barnesmore Gap on every one I'd call
There beyond the Blue Stack Mountains in the town of
Donegal

Oh Donegal I miss you and I'll never understand
Why I left you for these foreign lands against my heart's
command
Whatever fortune comes my way whatever may befall
I know I'll make my final destination Donegal

I would make my way from Malin to Bundoran through Raphoe
Or Portsalon down to Killybegs by Cresslough and Dungloe
I'd wander round by Barnesmore Gap on every one I'd call
There beyond the Blue Stack Mountains in the town of
Donegal
I know I'll make my final destination Donegal

" 'Destination Donegal' is a song written by Johnny McCauley. Donegal people have been singing it for as long as I can remember, especially when they are away from home. I think anybody who goes away from Ireland and Donegal leaves with the intention that one day they will return home. This is the sentiment in the song."

PLANE LANDING AT CARRICKFIN, MY LOCAL AIRPORT

OUTSIDE THE COPE IN KINCASSLAGH, WHERE I USED TO WORK

MY DONEGAL SHORE

Johnny McCauley

Oh I know it's not right, reminiscing tonight
Of days that are gone and returning no more
For the girl I dream of, has another man's love
Far, far away on a Donegal shore

But why should I care for she's happy o'er there
She may have children, she may be wealthy or poor
But I can't help my dreams of what might have been
If I stayed at home on my Donegal shore

Now it's winter time there, all the trees will be bare
And the rain clouds will darken my native Gweedore
But if that girl I could hold every raindrop would be gold
It could fall all around us on my Donegal shore

Now there's no one to blame but before she took his name
When she told me she loved him, it hurt to the core
But I could never descend, to be only her friend
So I left her there on my Donegal shore

Now it's winter time there, all the trees will be bare
And the rain clouds will darken my native Gweedore
But if that girl I could hold, every raindrop would be gold
It could fall all around us on my Donegal shore
But if that girl I could hold, every rain drop would be gold
It could fall all around us on my Donegal shore

"The first time I heard this song I was in a band with my sister Margaret (Margo). After a dance one night we were sitting around and a girl called Bridie Cahill from Kerry got up and sang 'My Donegal Shore'. It had been recorded at that time by Irish singing star Big Tom, but I hadn't heard him sing it. Bridie had a lovely singing voice, a really traditional sound, and I was captivated by her singing. From then on I sang it myself. I never thought it would mean so much to me but when I came to record for the first time it was the song I chose to do, just because I loved it. It made such a difference to my career; it opened up all the doors that I needed at the time. So it is a very special song for me. It was written by Johnny McCauley, who originally came from Derry but who now lives in London."

SUNSET IN KINCASSLAGH

17

HOME TO DONEGAL

P. Cavanagh

The lights of London are far behind
The thoughts of homeland are crowding my mind
Familiar places come into view
I see my home now soon I'll see you

We'll talk to the old folk, they're getting on
Treat them to late nights, sing a few songs
We'll talk of the neighbours and life in the town
There is so much to tell them, the days fly around

This is my homeland, the place I was born in
No matter where I go it's in my soul
My feet may wander a thousand places
But my heart will lead me back home to my Donegal

And then tomorrow we'll take a walk
Down to St Mary's to a sheltered spot
We'll kneel and pray there for the ones who have gone
And hope that they are proud of their wandering son

This is my homeland the place I was born in
No matter where I go it's in my soul
My feet may wander a thousand places
But my heart will lead me back home to my Donegal

This is my homeland the place I was born in
No matter where I go it's in my soul
My feet may wander a thousand places
But my heart will lead me back home to my Donegal
Yes my heart will lead me back to my Donegal

" 'Home to Donegal' has become an anthem. It is the most recent of many Donegal songs, written by a man called Patsy Kavanagh. Again it has been recorded by many, many people but I like to think that I added something special to it. I hope I did. I do it in almost all my shows. Just to hear people singing and joining in with the chorus is incredible, be it in London or Sydney or wherever; it has been a tremendous song. "

MYSELF AND ERRIGAL, NEAR CROLLY, DONEGAL   19

THE TOWNS I LOVE SO WELL

Although I grew up in a village, I have always loved the excitement and buzz of going to town. The first one I remember going to was Dungloe, a small town just down the road from where we lived. For me that was a real treat, but then we went further and visited Derry and later I got to see our capital, Dublin. Compared to our village, Dublin was a huge city full of bustle and life, but at that time it also had a faded small-town feel about it. Dublin is also a very elegant city, full of character, perhaps as a result of the fine Georgian architecture that seems to set the tone of the Dublin streets. Now Dublin, like all our towns, is expanding rapidly and growing in these 'Celtic Tiger' boom years. It is now, once again, one of the prime vibrant leading cities of Europe, as it actually was when all those fine buildings, like the Custom House, were originally built. In the rush for modernism or progress, I just hope that we can hold on to these treasures and to some of the values of the past, to keep Dublin and our other great cities and towns individual, Irish and unique. Great towns to visit now and in the future.

DUBLIN IN THE RARE AULD TIMES

Pete St John

Raised on songs and stories heroes of renown
The passing tales and glories, that once was Dublin town
The hallowed halls and houses, the haunting children's rhymes
That once was Dublin City in the rare auld times

Ring a Ring a Rosie, as the light declines
I remember Dublin City, in the rare auld times

My name it is Sean Dempsey as Dublin as can be
Born hardly lit in Pimlico in a house that's ceased to be
By trade I was a cooper lost out to redundancy
Like my house that fell to progress my trade's a memory
I courted Peggy Dignan, as pretty as you please
A roving child of Mary, from the rebel Liberties
I lost her to a student chap, with skin as black as coal
When he took her off to Birmingham, she took away my soul

Ring a Ring a Rosie, as the light declines
I remember Dublin City, in the rare auld times

The years have made me bitter, the gargle's dimmed my brain
Because Dublin keeps on changing and nothing seems the same
The pillar and the Met have gone the Royal long since
pulled down
As the grey unyielding concrete makes a city of our town
Fare thee well sweet Anna Liffey, I can no longer stay
And watch the new glass cages spring up along the quay
My mind's too full of memories, too old to hear new chimes
I'm a part of what was Dublin in the rare auld times

Ring a Ring a Rosie, as the light declines
I remember Dublin City, in the rare auld times
Ring a Ring a Rosie, as the light declines
I remember Dublin City, in the rare auld times

"Dublin has become one of Europe's most fashionable cities but to me its real charm is its people. They have a wonderful sense of humour and are incredibly warm. The real 'Dub' is as good as you could ever hope to meet. Dublin is a lovely city to walk around. For a capital city, it is so accessible. To wander down Grafton Street any afternoon and listen to the musicians and singers busking is an experience that, if you visit Ireland, you should not miss. If you get the opportunity, continue on and weave your way through to the rejuvenated Temple Bar area, cross the Halfpenny Bridge, and walk along the quays to O'Connell Street. If you walk up towards the historic General Post Office, where our Independence as a nation was declared in 1916, you can see the spot where Nelson's pillar once stood, now replaced with a modern spire. Then turn left into Henry Street, and on the right-hand side see the Moore Street traders. It's another experience you should not miss because these people are the real heart and soul of Dublin."

DUBLIN'S NORTH WALL QUAY, 2007

FROM THE TOP OF NELSON'S PILLAR, DUBLIN 1965. NELSON WAS LIBERATED IN 1966 BY A BOMB!

THE TOWN I LOVED SO WELL

Phil Coulter

In my memory I will always see
The town that I have loved so well
Where our school played ball by the gas-yard wall
And we laughed through the smoke and the smell
Going home in the rain running up the dark lane
Past the jail and down beside the fountain
Those were happy days in so many, many ways
In the town I loved so well

In the early morning the shirt factory horn
Called women from Creggan, the Moor and the Bog
While the men on the dole played a mother's role
Fed the children and then walked the dog
And when times got tough, there was just about enough
And they saw it through without complaining
For deep inside was a burning pride
In the town I loved so well

There was music there in the Derry air
Like a language that we could all understand
I remember the day when I earned my first pay
When I played in a small pickup band
There I spent my youth and to tell you the truth
I was sad to leave it all behind me
For I'd learned about life and I'd found a wife
In the town I loved so well

But when I returned how my eyes have burned
To see how a town could be brought to it's knees
By the armoured cars and the bombed out bars
And the gas that hangs on to every breeze
Now the army's installed by that old gas-yard wall
And the damned barbed wire gets higher and higher
With their tanks and guns, oh my God, what have they done?
To the town I loved so well

Now the music's gone but they carry on
For their spirit's been bruised, never broken
They'll not forget but their hearts are set
On tomorrow and peace once again
For what's done is done and what's won is won
And what's lost is lost and gone forever
I can only pray for a bright brand new day
In the town I loved so well

"'The Town I Loved So Well' is probably one of the greatest songs ever written about Ireland. It talks about the struggles Derry and its people faced through The Troubles and the resilience of the people. How their lives continued and how, despite much adversity, they seemed to have hope for the future, when I'm sure hope was something that was very, very hard to come by. They saw it through with great dignity. From my own point of view, we used to go on holidays to Derry every summer, when I was a child. We used to go on Anthony McGinley's bus. It would be going to Scotland and we would go to Derry on it. We went to a friend of my mother's called Leslie, and we stayed in Westland Avenue off the Lecky Road. It was the first place I saw swings and a roundabout in a park. I was impressed by the majestic sight of St Eugene's Cathedral, towering above the whole place. And another thing that fascinated me was the sight of a man in a van coming around selling lemonade. I'd never experienced that at home in Kincasslagh. Derry has always been a very special place and when I do shows there today I feel like I'm at home."

ST EUGENE'S CATHEDRAL, DERRY

DEAR OLD GALWAY TOWN

Rita Skerrit

I have travelled all round Ireland
From Dublin to Mayo
From Donegal to Kerry, from Leitrim to Sligo
But in all the miles I've travelled
All the roads that I've been down
There's one place I remember best
That's dear old Galway Town

If you ever go to Galway
And just walk down by the sea
I'm sure you will understand
Why it means so much to me
You see the smiling faces
Of the people all around
I'll not forget the folks I met
In dear old Galway Town

When I go across to England
And meet the people there
There's some from Cork and Wexford
And others are from Clare
Each one of them are friendly
But I have always found
You could not meet no nicer folk
Than those from Galway town

If you ever go to Galway
And just walk down by the sea
I'm sure you will understand
Why it means so much to me
You see the smiling faces
Of the people all around
I'll not forget the folks I met
In dear old Galway Town
No I'll not forget the folks I met
In dear old Galway Town

"I recorded this song, written by Rita Skerrit, many years ago. Margaret, my sister, had recorded it before me. I have mixed emotions when I think about Galway because I went to college there and I was not at all happy. I don't think it had anything to do with Galway. It's just that the college life didn't appeal to me. I stayed with some fantastic people called Pat and Sean Nugent in Renmore, and had great friends in Mary Teresa and Art Friel, who couldn't have made me more at home. But somehow I couldn't settle. When I think of Galway now I try not to think of those days, but rather I think of it being a very vibrant city. It is a city but somehow it has a town feel about it. There are wonderful seascapes. It is quite mesmerizing to walk and gaze on Galway Bay."

MY SISTER MARGO AND MYSELF
IN GALWAY CITY WHEN I WAS 8

KYLEMORE ABBEY, CO. GALWAY

LIMERICK YOU'RE A LADY

Denis Allen

Limerick you're a lady
Your Shannon waters tears of joy that flow
The beauty that surrounds you
I'll take it with me love where e'er I go
While waking in the arms of distant waters
A new day finds me far away from home
Then Limerick you're my lady
The one true love that I have ever known

As children you and I spent endless days of fun
In winter's snow or summer's golden sun
We fished in silver streams, the fabric of my dreams
Was fashioned by your loveliness and so I have to say:

Limerick you're a lady
Your Shannon waters tears of joy that flow
The beauty that surrounds you
I'll take it with me love where e'er I go
While waking in the arms of distant waters
A new day finds me far away from home
Then Limerick you're my lady
The one true love that I have ever known

A gift that time has made for travellers on their way
Seeking out the beauty of our lands
A shrine where children pray, and bells ring out to say
Thank God we're living just to feel the freedom of each day
Limerick you're a lady
Your Shannon waters tears of joy that flow
The beauty that surrounds you
I'll take it with me love where e'er I go
While waking in the arms of distant waters
A new day finds me far away from home

Then Limerick you're my lady
The one true love that I have ever known
While walking in the arms of distant waters
A new day finds me far away from home
And Limerick you're my lady
The one true love that I have ever known
The one true love that I have ever known

"Limerick is another Irish city that has been rejuvenated in the last decade thanks to the booming economy. Of course, it enjoys a wonderful national asset as the majestic River Shannon runs through it. That's a bonus for any city: Dublin has the Liffey and Cork has the Lee and they are all the richer for them. It was the singer and songwriter Denis Allen who penned this tribute to Limerick. It's a great ballad and it travels well. I was surprised that it was hugely popular when I included it in my shows around England."

"Limerick is another Irish city that has been rejuvenated in the last decade thanks to the booming economy. Of course, it enjoys a wonderful national asset as the majestic River Shannon runs through it."

ANY TIPPERARY TOWN

Johnny McCauley

Are you going across to Ireland?
Will you take me in your car?
And I'm sure you'll find my conversation sound
I can pay my way entirely, I'll enjoy your company
Leave me off at any Tipperary town

Sure there's Cashel, Tip and Lora
Or Boris or Flokeen
You can leave me where I have never been before
In Roscrea, Dundrum or Carrick in Thurles or Clonmell
Or my birthplace by the town of Templemore

Leave me on the road to Nenagh
Here the rippling Shannon call
Where the Arra mountains join the Silvermines
I'd be happy too in Cahir where the Galty shadows fall
I'm at home in any Tipperary town

I relive again the memories of times I used to know
When I let the wandering thoughts invade my mind
And the little town of Emly I lived so long ago
I rue the day I left them all behind

Leave me on the road to Neeagh
Here the rippling Shannon call
Where the Arra Mountains join the Silvermines
I'd be happy too in Cahir where the Galty shadows fall
I'm at home in any Tipperary town
I'm at home in any Tipperary town

"Tipperary is a county that in recent times is more important than it's ever been to me. My best friend, Josephine Bourke, comes from Cappaghwhite in Tipperary, and it was always special for that reason. And of course my wife, Majella, comes from Thurles in County Tipperary. This song was written by Johnny McCauley and he pays tribute to a great county. It has got fantastic scenery, the mountains and the lowlands, everything you could possibly want. I just can't say enough about it."

CAHIR CASTLE

A NEW FOAL NEAR BANSHA

BELFAST

A. Quinn

Of all the places I have been
There's only one to fill my dreams
The place that lingers in my mind
Is the town I left behind
I've been away now for too many years
I've read all the papers they told of your tears
Though I've left you with a heart that's been torn
I'm coming home now to the place I was born

That's Belfast you called to me. When I am far away
I think of thee, your Black Mountains, Cave Hill, City Hall
Shaw's Bridge, River Lagan, I'm going home to them all

I'll meet friends and relations each one I'll embrace
We'll pass round the pictures, which time can't erase
And it won't be long now 'til I see them all
Then I'll walk round the old streets and good times I'll recall

In Belfast you called to me. When I am far away
I think of thee. Your Black Mountains, Cave Hill, City Hall
Shaw's Bridge, River Lagan, I'm going home to them all

That's Belfast, you called to me. When I am far away
I think of thee. Your Black Mountains, Cave Hill, City Hall
Shaw's Bridge, River Lagan, I'm going home to them all

"'Belfast' is a song written relatively recently in the last twenty years by a man named Quinn from the group Barnbrack. It's a fantastic song that's up there with the best of the ballads. Whenever I sing it, the imagery of the chorus, with the mentions of Shaw's Bridge, The Black Mountains and Cave Hill, transports me to Belfast. I am sure that if you come from Belfast and are away it would transport you back too. It deals with The Troubles with lines like 'I left you with a heart that's been torn' or 'I've read all the papers that told of your tears.' It is very apparent that even if people never return, nothing can take away from their fond memories: 'We'll pass around the pictures, which time can't erase.' But it is also hopeful as there is the line, 'I'm going home to them all.' Now that the peace has come many Belfast people are thankfully returning home. This is all in the song 'Belfast'."

A VIEW OF CAVE HILL

HIGH STREET, BELFAST.

MAIN PHOTO : BELFAST ABOVE THE THE WATERFRONT CONCERT HALL WHERE I PLAY
BOTTOM: ME, A BELFAST STREET AT THE ULSTER FOLK AND TRANSPORT MUSEUM

HOME TOWN ON THE FOYLE

Johnny McCauley

As the train pulls out today from Derry City
A thousand memories linger in my mind
Why do I need to go? It's such a pity
And all the dear old friends I leave behind

As I gaze beyond the harbour I'm recalling
Familiar names like Doherty and Coyle
Through misty eyes I see the teardrops falling
Goodbye to my old hometown on the Foyle

The spire of St Eugene's seems to vanish
In the distance o'er the city way on high
My childhood thoughts I never want to vanish
When I wondered if it reaches to the sky

Many thousand miles I'll travel on my journey
To a new home on the wild Australian soil
But never can I hope to lose the yearning
To return to my old home town on the Foyle

No never can I hope to loose the yearning
To return to my old hometown on the Foyle

"This is another song written by Johnny McCauley. It is of course about Derry. Johnny McCauley must go down as one of the writers who has most ink in his pen when it comes to writing songs, as he wrote so many, over 80 I believe. I am grateful to have been able to do so many of them, as you can discover in this book. 'Home Town On The Foyle' is an emigration song again, as so many left on the 'scotch boat' to find work in Scotland, while others left by train to connect with the boat trains for England. Derry people are a very proud people, but it's not a selfish pride but a great shared pride, not a pride belonging to 'me' but a pride belonging to 'us' and that's always apparent in Derry. Derry people are rightly proud of their home town on the Foyle."

"Derry people are a very proud people, but it's not a selfish pride but a great shared pride..."

PRETTY LITTLE GIRL FROM OMAGH

Johnny McCauley

Way up in the north in old Tyrone
There's a pretty little girl I call my own
She's the sweetest rose Ireland's ever grown
And sure as the moon and stars above
I'm falling head over heels in love
With a pretty little girl from Omagh
In the county of Tyrone

There's cute little girls in old Strabane
They're just as pretty in Monaghan
This to every roving eye is known
But I guess that I'd be out of bounds
'Cos there between the northern towns
There's a pretty little girl from Omagh
In the county of Tyrone

She wears my ring and tells her friends
She's going to marry me
Best of all she tells them all
She's as happy as can be, oh lucky me
Well I don't know what she's done to me
There's nothing else my eyes can see
But a pretty little girl from Omagh
In the county of Tyrone

'Twas down in the south in old Tramore
I recall the yellow dress she wore
She strolled along the shore there all alone
But I guess it was my lucky day
When she came there on holiday
My pretty little girl from Omagh
In the county of Tyrone

She wears my ring and tells her friends
She's going to marry me
Best of all she tells them all
She's as happy as can be, oh lucky me
Well I don't know what she's done to me
There's nothing else my eyes can see
But a pretty little girl from Omagh
In the county of Tyrone
My pretty little girl from Omagh
In the county of Tyrone

" 'Pretty Little Girl From Omagh' is a great up-tempo song. It is a fun song to sing and for Irish people it is known the length and breadth of the country and would have been a great song in the dance hall days. The days in the 1960s and '70s when the great 'ballrooms of romance' were such an important part of the fabric of Irish popular culture for my generation and the generation before. This was the great 'showband' era before the discos killed them off in the '70s. I'd say half the country probably met their partners at one of these huge dance halls and there seemed to be one at almost every crossroads. They were great times and when I started out it was in the last days of the dance-hall era but I remember loving playing at them or going to them with friends. The Fiesta in Letterkenny was a fantastic purpose-built dance hall that was not too far for us. 'Pretty Little Girl From Omagh' would have been played at them all to get the girls moving on the dance floor."

FIESTA BALLROOM, LETTERKENNY

THESE ARE MY MOUNTAINS

I grew up with Errigal Mountain always watching over me and I love the majesty of our great mountains. Ireland is blessed with so many different mountain ranges with such wonderfully evocative names that capture the imagination: the Galty Mountains, MacGillycuddy's Reeks, the Blackstairs Mountains, the Knockmealdown Mountains, the Ballyhoura Mountains, the Derryveagh Mountains, the Twelve Pins, the Slieve Mish Mountains and, of course, the legendary Mountains of Mourne, known from the song all over the world.

Individual Mountains form part of the ancient history and legend of the country. Carrauntoohil near Killarney is our highest, while Mount Brandon, Slieve Donard, Croagh Patrick, Slievnamon, the Great Sugar Loaf, Lugnaquilla, Ben Bulben and so many more with great names are immortalised in songs, poetry and stories.

Our mountains are truly spectacular, especially as their moods change with the seasons and the weather. I go all over the world now but always think that our mountains are the best.

KILLARY HARBOUR – LEENANE, CO. GALWAY

THESE ARE MY MOUNTAINS

J. Copeland

For fame and for fortune
I've wandered the earth
But now I've returned to the land of my birth
I've brought back my treasures
But only to find
They're less than the pleasures
I first left behind

For these are my mountains
And this is my glen
The days of my childhood
I see them again
No land ever claimed me
Though far did I roam
For these are my mountains
And I'm going home

The stream by the road sings
At my going by
The lark overhead wings a
A welcoming cry
The lake where the trout lies
Once more I will see
For it's there that my heart lies
It's there I must be

Kind faces will meet me
And welcome me in
And oh how they will greet me
Back home again
This night round the fire side
Old songs will be sung
At last I'll be hearing my own mother's tongue

For these are my mountains
And this is my glen
The days of my childhood
I see them again
No land ever claimed me
Though far did I roam

For these are my mountains
And I'm going home
For these are my mountains
And I have come home

"Well I know that this song is actually based on a traditional Scottish song but the words touched me and as I come from a county with some spectacular mountains it seemed like I could adopt it as my own. I am sure the Scots have taken lots of our Irish songs and claimed them as their own, so I hope I'll be forgiven for it's inclusion here. I recorded it for my second album 'The Two Sides' in 1985. It was also on my 'Irish Album' in 2002, so the precedent is well established. Scotland has always played an important role in my career, so it is good to share this song. I got the song from Scottish songwriter Jimmy Copeland."

LOUGH TAY, CO. WICKLOW

THE BLUE HILLS OF BREFFNI

D. O'Brien

The blue hills of Breffni shining in the sun
Scenes that I knew so long ago
When in my boyhood barefoot I would run
Through the fields and the woodlands I would go

Down by the river there is an old swimming hole
Where we laughed and played the summer days away
And home in the evening with the sun sinking low
In the blue hills of Breffni far away

Far away, far away, blue Hills of Breffni far away
Old memories burning soon I'll be returning
To my blue hills of Breffni far away

Old thatched cottage standing by the stream
Winter nights of story and of song
And the sound of the fiddle that my father used to play
And the music echoed as we sang along

Neighbours would gather round the old turf fire
And they talked about the heroes of the day
Life was all for living in the days when we were young
In the blue hills of Breffni far away

Far away, far away, blue Hills of Breffni far away
Old memories burning soon I'll be returning
To my blue hills of Breffni far away

I had a sweetheart she was young and fair
She cared not that I had no wealth or fame
We'd go walking hand in hand along the leafy lanes
To the old oak tree where once I carved her name

There we made our promises that we would never part
And our love would last for ever and a day
But I went a roving and left my love behind
In the Blue Hills of Breffni far away

Far away, far away, blue Hills of Breffni far away
Old memories burning soon I'll be returning
To my blue hills of Breffni far away
To my blue hills of Breffni far away

"This song by Denis O'Brien was on my second album in 1985 and was a very popular song for dancing and is almost the opposite side of the coin to the sentiment of Ballyhoe. In this song the young man has gone away having made the promises to his sweetheart that they would not part but he 'went a roving and left his love behind'. But there is hope in the last chorus as he says 'old memories burning soon I'll be returning to my Blue Hills of Breffni far away'. He does not mention the sweetheart though, it is just the mountains he misses. The Sligo Leitrim border is a very beautiful part of Ireland."

THE GREAT SUGAR LOAF, CO. WICKLOW

THE COOMERA MOUNTAINS, CO. WATERFORD

THE GREEN HILLS OF SLIGO

D. Henry

I'm leaving dear old Ireland I can no longer stay
I have decided to sail west o'er to the USA
There are many different reasons that have urged me on
to go
And leave the place where I was born round the Green
Hills of Sligo

Although I hate to leave this land where I have lived for
many years
I find that I must emigrate though my eyes are full of tears
For there's nothing left for me to do no future that I know
And so I have to bid fare well to the Green Hills of Sligo

I know my friends will disagree and Father Brown will too
They'll all be trying to tell me that the day I leave I'll rue
My poor old mother will be sad when I tell her I must go
And leave the place where I was born round the Green
Hills of Sligo

I'll write a letter now and then to all my friends so dear
I'll tell them all the things I can about my lifetime here
And when I long for memories and days of long ago
I'll think about the neighbours around the Green Hills
of Sligo

Although I hate to leave this land where I have lived for
many years
I find that I must emigrate though my eyes are filled
with tears
For there's nothing left for me to do, no future that I know
And so I have to bid fare well to the Green Hills of Sligo
And so I have to bid fare well to the Green Hills of Sligo

"Sligo is the neighbouring county to Donegal and actually Mick's father's family came from Sligo town. The song was one of the first I ever recorded in about 1984. I was attracted to this song because I love the tune and sentiment. Like so many Irish songs, it's about migration. It explains how the poor guy in the song had no choice but to leave his beloved Sligo in search of work. It was the story of many, many Irish people. They didn't always want to go but they had no other option. Despite its sad theme, it has a lovely chorus: 'There are many different reasons to go.' Sometimes in these old songs I wonder if love had a part to play, be it forbidden or otherwise. Maybe it's the case in this one."

MOUNTAINS ON THE SLIGO/LEITRIM BORDER

THE MOUNTAINS OF MOURNE

Percy French

Oh Mary this London's a wonderful sight
With the people here working by day and by night
They don't sow potatoes nor barley nor wheat
But there's gangs of them digging for gold in the streets
At least when I asked them that's what I was told
So I just took a hand at this digging for gold
But for all that I found there I might as well be
Where the Mountains of Mourne sweep down to the sea

I believe that when writing a wish you expressed
As to how the fine ladies in London were dressed
Well, if you'll believe me when asked to a ball
Faith they don't wear a top to their dresses at all
Oh I've seen them myself and you could not in truth
Say if they were bound for a ball or a bath
Don't be starting them fashions now, Mary mo chroi
Where the Mountains of Mourne sweep down to the sea

You remember young Peter O'Loughlin, of course
Well he's over here at the head of the Force
Sure I met him today as I was crossing the Strand
And he stopped the whole street with one wave of his hand
And there we stood talking of days that are gone
While the whole population of London looked on
But for all his great powers he's wishful like me
To be back where the dark Mournes sweep down to the sea

There's beautiful girls here but ah never you mind
With beautiful shapes Nature never designed
And lovely complexions, all roses and cream
But O'Loughlin remarked with regard to the same
That if at those roses you venture to sip
The colours might all come away on your lips
So I'll wait for the wild rose that's waiting for me
Where the Mountains of Mourne sweep down to the sea

"This is another brilliant song by Percy French, and his tongue-in-cheek approach to writing is in evidence. The crowning glory of County Down is the Mountains of Mourne range, which sweep down to the sea. The local Slieve Donard Hotel is an impressive building, but it's almost nothing compared to the towering Mountains of Mourne. Sometimes I think, when I stand there, that incredible as the structure of this wonderful hotel is, the creation of God makes all man-made things pale into insignificance."

'WHERE THE MOUNTAINS OF MOURNE SWEEP DOWN TO THE SEA'

AMONG THE WICKLOW HILLS

Johnny McCauley

I've just received a letter from my home in Ireland
The scribble so familiar 'twas my mother's feeble hand
A house that rang with music and of laughter now is still
Dear Danny it's so lonely here, among the Wicklow Hills

As I gaze across the mountains I relive a moment's joy
The same old Wicklow Mountains where you rambled as a boy
Your photo as a child. That picture's by my bedside still
And each night I pray that you'll come back home
Among the Wicklow Hills

Do you remember long ago when in summer you would stroll?
Down where the crystal mountain streams to the Slaney
waters rolled?
Do you recall the young companion who talks about you still?
And do you know who, she is waiting too among the Wicklow
Hills?

The same old Wicklow Mountains where you rambled as a boy
Your photo as a child, that picture's by my bedside still
And each night I pray that you'll come back home
Among the Wicklow Hills

Yes, each night I'll pray that you'll come back home
Among the Wicklow Hills

"The beautiful county of Wicklow is known as the 'Garden of Ireland', and if you stand at Sally Gap and take a view over towards the coast you will be bewitched by the breathtaking sight. Glendalough is also beautiful. Bray is the seaside town and was very popular with Irish holidaymakers. I met an elderly couple from Dublin on a plane recently, and the man said they rented a house in Bray for their summer break. Now, of course, as the city sprawls outwards, it is almost part of Dublin. It is a picturesque county all year round. In the autumn it's particularly stunning when the leaves change colour."

NEAR LOUGH DAN, WICKLOW

LUGGALA ON THE BANKS OF LOUGH TAY. THE LAKE LOOKS LIKE A POOL OF GUINNESS
AND THE HOUSE BELONGS TO THE GUINNESS FAMILY

SLIEVENAMON

Charles J. Kickham

Alone, all alone, by the wave-washed strand
All alone in a crowded hall
The hall it is gay and the waves they are grand
But my heart sure is not here at all

It flies far away, by night and by day
To the times and the joys that are gone
And I never can forget the sweet maiden I met
In the valley near Slievenamon.

In the festive ball by the wave-washed shore
My restless spirit flies
My love, oh my love, shall I never see you more
Oh my land will you ever uprise

By night and by day I ever, ever pray
While lonely my life rolls on
To see our flag unrolled and my true love too enfold
In the valley near Slievenamon

It flies far away, by night and by day
To the times and the joys that are gone
And I never can forget the sweet maiden I met
In the valley near Slievenamon

"This is a huge ballad not only in Ireland, but especially for Tipperary people. In fact, it is recognised as the county anthem for the Tipperary sports enthusiasts. It can be heard at the big 'Tip' sporting fixtures for both Gaelic football and hurling. It was originally written by a patriot called Charles Kickham who was born near Slievenamon and died in 1882. He was a journalist and writer and later became a leading nationalist in Dublin. Slievenamon, which rises to 2,363 feet, is also known as the 'mountain of the women', so it is no surprise that the song means a great deal to the woman in my life, Majella, who is very proud of her Tipperary roots and loves the ballad. That makes the song even more important and emotional for me."

CELEBRATION

THE CRAIC: FUN, GAMES AND FESTIVALS.

An essential part of life in Ireland is enjoying the craic. The 'craic was mighty' is not a reference to excessive drug use, but a term heard often to express satisfaction with a party, festival, race meeting, social gathering or any place that people meet up to enjoy the company, the banter and the event. Generally, but not always, drink is taken, often the black stuff to relax the tongues. You don't have to search far in Ireland to find us enjoying the craic and visitors are always welcomed and encouraged to join in. In Ireland we are passionate about sport and love our own games of Hurling and Gaelic football, played out with fantastic all Ireland finals at the Citadel of Gaelic Games at Croke Park in Dublin. In 2007, history was made when the GAA allowed for the first time foreign games to be played upon the sacred pitch. There was a fantastic occasion when the Irish rugby team beat their old rivals England at Croke Park in front of a capacity crowd and a massive worldwide TV audience. Both the Irish and English national anthems were sung in an emotionally charged atmosphere, and were respected in sportsmanlike manner by the huge crowd of spectators. It was an incredible sporting occasion for everybody with great humour enjoyed by players, spectators and the thousands who could not get into the ground but who enjoyed the game in pubs and bars across Europe. Since then, soccer and other sports as well as rock concerts have taken place at Croke Park. In 1992, the Donegal Gaelic football team got into the All Ireland final for the first time and beat Dublin. The celebrations went on in Donegal for weeks and we were all so proud. There are thousands of festivals, fleadghs and sporting occasions where we enjoy ourselves and the craic. After a few pints of our national drink we often break into song. Joining in is obligatory for visitors!

TOP & MIDDLE: IT RAINED ON THE PARADE – ST PATRICK'S DAY IN CHARLESTOWN, CO. MAYO 2007
BOTTOM: SUNDAY GAELIC FOOTBALL AT THE FOOT OF SLIEVENAMON

MARY FROM DUNGLOE

Colm O'Laughlainn

Oh then fare thee well sweet Donegal,
The Rosses and Gweedore
I'm crossing the main ocean
Where the foaming billows roar
It breaks my heart from you to part
Where I spent many happy days
Farewell to kind relations
I am bound for Amerikay

Oh then Mary you're my heart's delight
My pride and only care
It was your cruel father
Would not let me stay there
But absence makes the heart grow fond,
And when I am over the main
May the Lord protect my darling girl
'Til I return again

Oh I wish I was in sweet Dungloe
And seated on the grass
And by my side a bottle of wine
And on my knee a lass
I'd call for liquor of the best
And I'd pay before I'd go
And I'd roll my Mary in my arms
In the town of sweet Dungloe

"'Mary from Dungloe' is a song that is very close to my heart. Dungloe is the nearest town to us at home. It's just six miles from Kincasslagh but it was quite an event to go to Dungloe when we were young. We travelled on the Swilly bus and you would have to spend the day in Dungloe as the bus didn't return until the evening. It would come at about a quarter to two. In true Irish fashion it would never be early, whatever way it would be late.

The song 'Mary from Dungloe' was inspired by a forbidden love. A local man fell in love with a girl called Mary Gallagher, and her family thought he wasn't good enough for her. She then emigrated to New Zealand. On the boat to New Zealand she met a man called Daniel Egan, whom she married. She died shortly after her first child was born and the child then died at six months. It's an incredible story of how much control a family had over who a son or daughter should marry in an era when you would have thought there would be no class distinction. I actually visited the grave where Mary was buried in Gisburn, New Zealand.

The Mary from Dungloe is also a popular local festival, this year 2007 being its 40th anniversary."

A BRIDE NEAR KINVARA, AUGUST 2006

SHE MOVED THROUGH THE FAIR

Traditional

My young love said to me 'my mother won't mind
And my father won't slight you for your lack of kind'
And she stepped away from me and this she did say
'Oh it will not be long love 'til our wedding day'

She stepped away from me and she moved through the fair
And fondly I watched her move here and move there
And she made her way homeward with one star awake
As the swan in the evening moves over the lake

The people were saying that no two were e'er wed
But one has a sorrow that never was said
And I smiled as she passed with her goods and her gear
And that was the last I saw of my dear

On the last time I saw her when she moved through the fair
I had gazed as the sunlight did dance through her hair
But the winds in the rushes their secret do keep
Like the waves on the shoreline, that my love's asleep

Last night I did dream that my love she came in
And so softly she came that her feet made no din
And she laid her hand on me and smiling did say
'It will not be long, love, 'til our wedding day'

"'She Moved Through The Fair' has a haunting tune and the words will be known by anybody with Irish connections. I can remember it from my childhood. It is a very old and traditional love song and nobody knows who wrote the original upon which, the song we know now, is based and I assume the basis was a very old handed down air. Many of these traditional songs have such beautiful tunes, like the melody for Boulavogue, they are so plaintive and emotional. In 1909 a man called Padraic Colum wrote the words based on a fragment of two lines of the old song whilst the melody came from Donegal. That's why it is so good! A song collector called Herbert Hughes had found it and asked Padraic Colum to complete the words from the last two lines that were left. So he had to work backwards to create something with the original feel. He did a wonderful job. Years ago a travelling singer called Margaret Barry was known for doing it on RTE radio, Mary O'Hara from Sligo played the harp and sang it too and it has since been recorded by many singers. A few years ago Sinead O'Connor did a moving version for the film about Michael Collins."

MOUNT STEWART GARDENS, CO. DOWN

THE FIELDS OF ATHENRY

Pete St John

By a lonely prison wall I heard a young girl call
'Michael they have taken you away
For you stole Trevelyn's corn
So the young might see the morn
Now a prison ship lies waiting in the bay'

Low lie the fields of Athenry
Where once we watched the small free birds fly
Our love was on the wing, we had dreams and songs to sing
It's so lonely 'round the fields of Athenry

By a lonely prison wall I heard a young man calling
'Nothing matters, Mary, when you're free
Against the famine and the Crown I rebelled, they cut me down
Now you must raise our child with dignity'

Low lie the fields of Athenry
Where once we watched the small free birds fly
Our love was on the wing, we had dreams and songs to sing
It's so lonely 'round the fields of Athenry

By a lonely harbour wall she watched the last star falling
As that prison ship sailed out against the sky
For she'll live in hope and pray
For her love in Botany Bay
It's so lonely 'round the fields of Athenry

Low lie the fields of Athenry
Where once we watched the small free birds fly
Our love was on the wing, we had dreams and songs to sing
It's so lonely 'round the fields of Athenry

"Although it sounds like an old song that has been handed down for generations, it was actually written in the 1970s by Dublin songwriter Pete St John. The plaintive and moving lyrics relate, in the first person, the plight of the potato famine and the cruel punishment that faced any man who stole corn to feed his starving family. The prisoner in the song is deported to Botany Bay penal colony in Australia, leaving his family to starve. The British civil servant Trevelyan is named in the song. He is blamed for the lack of the Government's response to the crisis. By not recognising the consequences of the failure of the potato crop, he and the administration inadvertently caused what could be called genocide in part of the British Isles. It is incredible in my mind that this slow 'folk' ballad has been adopted as a sports anthem by Gaelic games supporters in Galway and by the Munster, London Irish and Irish National Rugby teams. To hear it being sung by huge crowds in massive stadiums is very stirring and emotional."

FORTY SHADES OF GREEN

Well, if you know nothing else about Ireland you must know that it is green! Johnny Cash in his classic song says there are forty shades but I think he was wrong – there are more. Green is our national colour. It had huge significance in the penal times when it was forbidden to show any signs of Irishness, so later we all grew up knowing the song 'The Wearing Of The Green' as a statement of national pride. When landing in Ireland from travel to other countries, it is always amazing to see all the different shades of green in the Irish landscape. Every field seems to have a different hue like a giant paint colour chart. I suppose that it is the abundance of water in our rivers and lakes fed by the rain. How many times are we told it is a 'soft day' when actually it is bucketing down?! This keeps our grass well watered and verdant green, which makes our landscape so beautiful. The climate does seem to be changing, though, and we have had some brilliant hot weather recently. I was in Killarney at Easter in 2007 when there was two weeks of 'summer' weather, with not a drop of rain. June made up for that by being the wettest for 70 years, so I think our very special green fields are safe for now.

THE LAKE AT MOUNT TEMPLE, CO. SLIGO

40 SHADES OF GREEN FROM A PLANE WINDOW

FORTY SHADES OF GREEN

Johnny Cash

I close my eyes and picture
The emerald of the sea
From the fishing boats at Dingle
To the shores of Donaghadee
I miss the river Shannon
And the folks at Skibbereen
The moorlands and the meadows
With their forty shades of green.

But most of all I miss a girl in Tipperary town
And most of all I miss her lips
As soft as eiderdown
Again I want to see and do
The things we've done and seen
Where the breeze is sweet as Shalimar
And there's forty shades of green

I wish that I could spend an hour
At Dublin's churning surf
I'd love to watch the farmers
Drain the bog and spade the turf
To see again the thatching
Or the straw the women glean
I'd walk from Cork to Larne to see
The forty shades of green

But most of all I miss a girl in Tipperary town
And most of all I miss her lips
As soft as eiderdown
Again I want to see and do
The things we've done and seen
Where the breeze is sweet as Shalimar
And there's forty shades of green
Where the breeze is sweet as Shalimar
And there's forty shades of green

"Johnny Cash, the great and sadly missed country singer, was in Ireland in the early 1960s and fell in love with the country. He was so impressed with the scenic countryside, which looked so different from his native America, and he was so moved by the appreciation shown to him by his Irish fans that he was inspired to write this classic song. Now both the song and his description of Ireland are embedded in our culture. His lyrics and imagery are perfect at reflecting the time when he wrote the song, capturing an Ireland that had not changed for years. The song immortalises the good old days of thatching, cutting straw and a time when 'the farmers drain the bogs and spade the turf'. It was the 'Man In Black' who made Ireland famous for being 'forty shades of green' and although there have been countless recordings; I just love to hear the Johnny Cash original version. Partly because of that I recorded the song very early on in my career."

FISHING BOATS – KNIGHTSTOWN, VALENTIA ISLAND

THE BEARA PENINSULAR – HALF IN CO. CORK, HALF IN CO. KERRY

PAT MURPHY'S MEADOW

Traditional

The autumn days are here again
And the night winds chilly blow
The woodlands turn to golden hue
And the harvest moon's aglow
To hear again of days long past
To come no more I know
When I mowed Pat Murphy's meadow
In the sunny long ago.

I see again the ocean and the distant sails afar
As the maidens in the meadow strike up 'Dark Lochnagar'
There was music soft and tender
In the winds that whisper low
When I mowed Pat Murphy's meadow
In the sunny long ago

Where are the happy boys and girls
Who danced the gay quadrilles?
And the singer who warbled sweetly
'The Burning Granite Mill'?
To hear again at sunset
'Where Sweet Afton Water's Flow'
When I mowed Pat Murphy's meadow
In the sunny long ago

Those days are but a memory
Like the snows of a yesteryear
And when evening shades are falling
All alone I'll shed a tear
On my cheeks I feel the soft touch
Of the winds that whispered low
When I mowed Pat Murphy's meadow
In the sunny long ago

When I mowed Pat Murphy's meadow
Of the winds that whispered low
When I mowed Pat Murphy's meadow
In the sunny long ago
When I mowed Pat Murphy's meadow

"I love this ballad as it is almost in the style of Sean-nos singing. Some people just love the sound of Sean-nos singers but others find the sound of the unaccompanied voice performing slow ballads, usually in the Irish language, less appealing. I think that there is a purity to the Sean-nos style. Even if you don't have the Irish language, the emotion can still be felt, the words spring from the heart. There is a fantastic traditional group called Altan, who come from near my home place in Donegal and sometimes they perform in a Sean-nos style. 'Pat Murphy's Meadow' is a song that reminds me of that style of singing that I grew up hearing from my neighbours. It is a lovely ballad."

A MEADOW IN KILLARNEY, CO. KERRY

A MEADOW IN CO. KILDARE

THE ROADS OF KILDARE

John Duggan

Johnny was born in a mansion down in the county of Clare
Rosie was born by the roadside somewhere in County Kildare
Destiny brought them together on the road near Killorglin
One day 'neath her bright kilty shawl she was singing
And she stole his young heart away
For she sang...

Chorus
Meet me tonight by the campfire
Come with me over the hill
Let us be married tomorrow
Please let me whisper 'I will'
What if the neighbours are talking?
Who cares if your friends stop and stare?
You'll be proud to be married to Rosie
Who was reared on the roads of Kildare

Think of the parents who reared you
Think of the family name
How can you marry a gypsy?
Oh what a terrible shame
Parents and friends stop your pleading
Don't worry about my affairs
For I've fallen in love with a gypsy
Who was reared on the roads of Kildare
For she sang...

Repeat chorus

Johnny went down from his mansion
Just as the sun had gone down
Turning his back on his kinfolk
Likewise his dear native town
Facing the roads of old Ireland
With a gypsy he loved so sincere
When he came to the light of the campfire
These are the words he did hear
For she sang...

Repeat chorus

You'll be proud to be married to Rosie,
Who was reared on the roads of Kildare

"Although it seems as if the song has been around for ages it was written not very long ago. I just love it. There is a sense of romanticism in the perceived freedom of the Irish gypsy or travelling community, although the reality for the 'travellers' of today is that they have a very hard life. This song is pure fiction. A made-up story, with the young, well-to-do man leaving his mansion and heading off to meet his Rosie at her campfire, for a life of freedom on the road. The road shown in the picture is near the Curragh of Kildare, a region in Ireland famous for horseracing. When the picture was taken, just over the brow of the hill there was actually a travellers' camp where the families have probably come for many generations. Perhaps our 'Rosie' is one of them. The song has a great tune and it is such a good happy sing-along that I love performing it."

SHEEP ON THE CURRAGH

SUMMERTIME IN IRELAND

John Farry

I woke up this morning another sunny morning
Thinking gee it's good to be alive
Pulling back the curtains and knowing that for certain
It's going to be another lovely day

Strolling through the hedgerows my true love on my arm
Hear the song bird singing in the trees
Walking down the country lanes in the afternoon
Seeing the lambs a-playing in the fields

It's summer time again, the winter days are over
Flowers they are growing in the garden once again
The roses they are blooming the trees no longer bare
'Cos it's summer time in Ireland and I'm so glad to be there

If you're living here in Ireland it's sights like this you'll see
With scenery that is beyond compare
My favourite time of the year is when the song birds are here
The best of all the seasons I declare

It's summer time again, the winter days are over
Flowers they are growing in the garden once again
The roses they are blooming the trees no longer bare
Cos' it's summer time in Ireland and I'm so glad to be there

It's summer time again, the winter days are over
Flowers they are growing in the garden once again
The roses they are blooming the trees no longer bare
Cos' it's summer time in Ireland and I'm so glad to be there
It's summer time in Ireland and I'm so glad to be there

"A songwriter from Garrison in County Fermanagh, John Farry wrote this song, which I have performed from the very early days, when I started playing at dances. I love the song as the lyrics convey all the good feelings associated with a lovely summer's day; it is always really popular, when raising the tempo of the shows. John is an excellent songwriter, who has written for many singers including writing a Eurovision Song Contest entry, performed by my friend Marc Roberts in 1977. I have recorded about a dozen of his songs but 'Summertime In Ireland' is very special for me, as it was my first Number 1 hit in Ireland in 1987. I'll always be grateful for the boost the song gave to my career."

VIEW FROM GLANLEAM, VALENTIA ISLAND, CO. KERRY

A GARDEN GATE – ROSS CASTLE, OUGHTERARD, CO. GALWAY

THE GREEN GLENS OF ANTRIM

K. North

Far across yonder blue lies a true fairy land
With the sea rippling over the shingle and sand
Where the gay honeysuckle is luring the bee
And the green glens of Antrim are calling to me

Sure if only you knew how the light of the moon
Turns a blue Irish bay to a silver lagoon
You'd imagine the picture of heaven it would be
Where the green glens of Antrim are welcoming me

Soon I hope to return to my own Cushendall
'Tis the one place for me that can outshine them all
Sure I know every stone I recall every tree
Where the green glens of Antrim are heaven to me

Sure I'd be where the people are simple and kind
And amongst them there's one who's been, aye on my mind
Oh I'd pray that the world would in peace let me be
Where the green glens of Antrim are calling to me
Where the green glens of Antrim are calling to me

"'The Green Glens of Antrim' was written in 1950 by Kenneth North. It is a beautiful song, evocative of a beautiful place and describes the sentiment of a proud but homesick man thinking back to the place he misses. Like many of the songs in this book, it relates the feelings of a traveller who has left Ireland and longs to return to see the beautiful scenery of the 'Green Glens of Antrim' and to that one special person he has left behind in Cushendall. There are actually nine beautiful glens that lead out to the sea on the dramatic north coast of Ireland, carved out of the rock by glaciers thousands of years ago. Glenarm, Glencloy, Glenariff, Glenballyeamon, Glenaan, Glencorp, Glendun, Glenshesk and Glentaisie are their names. With individual characteristics, each is full of stories, legends and mythology. Despite having a coast road that is rated as being one of the most spectacular coast roads in the world, the Glens of Antrim have not changed very much over the years and they have not been over-commercialised by tourism. For a visitor today they are still very much the 'picture of heaven it could be, where the Green Glens of Antrim are calling to me'. It is such a beautiful song about a beautiful unspoilt part of our Island."

ANTRIM TOWN

PEACEFUL WATERS

In 1999, Mick had the idea of making a film called 'Peaceful Waters'. It involved me travelling on a boat down the newly opened Peace Canal, from the north to the south, as a celebration of the progress being made at the time on the peace process. I had driven past the rivers and lakes in this part of Ireland many times, but going slowly by canal boat was a revelation and a lot of fun. I realised that so much of our beautiful landscape is made up of spectacular rivers and lakes, some hidden and some in the middle of our towns. All over Ireland there are beautiful babbling streams, flowing rivers and crystal watered lakes and pools. These have inspired memories, poetry and songs as well as giving us fantastic places for swimming, boating and fishing or maybe just to enjoy the tranquillity of our peaceful waters.

ON THE BEARA PENINSULA NEAR LAURAGH, CO. KERRY

THE ISLE OF INNISFREE

Dick Farrelly

I've met some folks who say that I'm a dreamer
And I've no doubt there is truth in what they say
For sure a body's bound to be a dreamer
When all the things he loves are far away

And precious things are dreams unto an exile
They take him to a land across the sea
Especially when it happens he's an exile
From that dear lovely Isle of Innisfree

And when the moonlight peeps across the rooftops
Of this great city, wondrous though it be
I scarcely see the beauty or the magic
I'm once again back home in Innisfree

I wander o'er green hills and dreamy valleys
And find a peace no other land could know
I hear the birds make music fit for Angels
And then see the rivers lapping as they flow

And then into a humble shack I wander
My own sweet home and tenderly behold
The folks I love around the turf fire gathered
On bended knee the rosary is told

But dreams don't last though dreams are not forgotten
When we are back to stark reality
And though they pave the footpaths here with gold dust
I still would choose my Isle of Innisfree
I still would choose my Isle of Innisfree

"In the early 1950s Dick Farrelly, a Dublin policeman, wrote a song that found its way to Bing Crosby, whose recording of it became a million seller and one of his biggest hits. The song returns to that familiar theme of an emigrant pining for his homeplace and the home place in question this time is here in County Sligo, the beautiful Isle of Innisfree. The song was also used as the theme to the John Wayne film classic, THE QUIET MAN set in 'Inisfree' as the childhood village to which his American character, Sean Thornton, returns. However, the famous bridge location from which he is seen looking across to his old family home in his Hollywood 'Inisfree', is actually some miles away from Sligo, in the epic scenery of Connemara. This tranquil water scene is also made famous in the poem, THE LAKE ISLE OF INNISFREE by the famous Irish poet William Butler Yeats. He is buried near here under the shadow of Ben Bulben in Drumcliffe. I came here to Sligo to perform the song for my video Thoughts of Home in 1989, when Mick took the black and white picture and it has always been a favourite of mine."

"In the early 1950s Dick Farrelly, a Dublin policeman, wrote a song that found its way to Bing Crosby…"

THE QUIET MAN'S 'INISFREE' BRIDGE

BEN BULBEN

AN IRISH LULLABY
Traditional

Over in Killarney many years ago
My mother sang a song to me
In tones so sweet and low
Just a simple little ditty
In her good old Irish way
And I'd give the world if she could sing that song
For me today

Chorus
Toora loora looral
Toora loorali
Toora loora looral
Hush now don't you cry
Toora loora looral
Toora loorali
Toora looral looral
That's an Irish lullaby

Oft' in dreams I wander to that cot again
I feel her arms a hugging me as when she held me then
And I hear her voice a humming to me as in days of yorn
When she used to rock me fast asleep outside our
Cottage door

Repeat chorus

"There can hardly be a child born to Irish parents since 1944 who has not been lulled to sleep by the gentle 'Toora Loora Loora' of an 'Irish Lullaby', sung by their mother. I was no exception to this as it is probably the first song I ever heard, as my mother sang it to me as a child. The song reached its peak of popularity when Bing Crosby had a million selling Number 4 hit with his version from the film Going My Way (1944) and the popularity of the song in America resulted in its success around the world. The song was actually written in 1913 by James Royce Shannon for a musical called Shameen Dhu, or Black Jamie, which opened in New York in 1914. Shannon was an actor from Michigan who wrote songs for musicals and vaudeville singers and I guess from his name that he had an Irish background. Perhaps he got the 'Toora Loora' idea from an air his mother had sung to him as a child. It is a lovely and gentle song which I enjoyed recording and love to sing at my concerts."

A CIRCUS BIG TOP FROM A FAIRY RING IN KILLARNEY

THE LAKE IN KILLARNEY

THE BANKS OF MY OWN LOVELY LEE

J. Shanahan

How oft' do my thoughts in their fancy take flight
To the home of my childhood away
To the days when each patriot's vision seemed bright
E'er I dreamed that those joys should decay
When my heart was as light as the fair wind that blows
Down the Mardyke through each elm tree
Where I sported and played 'neath each green leafy shade
On the banks of my own lovely Lee
Where I sported and played 'neath each green leafy shade
On the banks of my own lovely Lee

And then in the springtime of laughter and song
Can I ever forget the sweet hours?
With the friends of my youth as we rambled along
'Mongst the green mossy banks and wild flowers
Then too, when the evening's sun sinking to rest
Sheds it's golden light over the sea
The maid with her lover the wild daisies pressed
On the banks of my own lovely Lee
The maid with her lover the wild daisies pressed
On the banks of my own lovely Lee

"The proud people of Cork consider that Cork City is the real capital of Ireland and when I sing this famous ballad at concerts in Cork it feels as if the roof will come off with the excitement of the audience as they sing the song. It is just so incredible. Cork City is the major city in the south west of Ireland. In fact 'Coraigh', the Irish name for Cork City, means a marshy boggy place but when it was drained the River Lee was split into two main streams that still run through the City, so that there are now lovely walks to be taken on the banks of the River Lee. These walks are known by all Cork people and that is why the song has such a powerful meaning for people who live there but also for those who came from Cork but who now live away. Courting couples would walk down the Mardyke, as mentioned in the song. There is also a recollection in the song: 'sported and played neath each green leafy shade', which is fitting as the song is now not just the anthem for a great city but has also been adopted by Cork fans at big sporting occasions. I love the song and have been singing it for a long time but I have also recently included it in a TV special for PBS television in America."

GOUGANE BARRA, CO. CORK

BALLYHOE

Eilish Boland

You told me that you would come back some day
To me in Ballyhoe
But never a word since you went away
From me so long ago
The hours are long the lonely days are drifting into years
Oh it's getting late, but I still wait
With eyes growing dim with tears

Oh do you remember the hawthorn bush
Where we gathered every spring?
Do you remember the reels we danced
Around the fairy ring?
And do you remember a promise made
Beneath the chestnut tree?
But best of all, my absent one
Do you remember me?

I wander along by the lakeside now
At sunset's early glow
Just thinking of all the dreams I dreamed
Of you so long ago
The whispers come the whispers go
They echo over the sea
That a foreign land and a foreign strand
Have stolen you from me

Oh do you remember the hawthorn bush
We gathered every spring
Do you remember the reels we danced
Around the fairy ring?
And do you remember a promise made
Beneath the chestnut tree?
But best of all, my absent one
Do you remember me?
But best of all, my absent one
Do you remember me?

"This is another great waltz song that I recorded for my first album. The song is different from some of the others in that it is written from the perspective of the person who is left behind in Ireland to the loved one who has emigrated. So many times those leaving must have made promises to return and they doubtless believed that they would return. They were invariably leaving because they had to and would have hoped to come back. The reality was that once settled in a new country with a job and new friends it was unlikely that they would come back and many never came back for years if at all. It must have been terribly hard to say goodbye at the Railway Station or bus stop knowing really that the promises would be broken and they may never see their sweetheart again."

MILL LANE, ULSTER FOLK MUSEUM

THE MEETING OF THE WATERS

Thomas Moore

There is not in this wide world a valley so sweet
As that vale in whose bosom the bright waters meet
Oh the last rays of feeling and life must depart
E'er the bloom of that valley shall fade from my heart

Yet it was not what nature had shed o'er the scene
The purest of crystal and brightest of green
'Twas not her soft magic of streamlet or hill
Oh no it was something more exquisite still

'Twas that the friends beloved of my heart were near
And they made every scene of beauty more dear
They could feel how the best charms of nature improve
When we view them reflected in those whom we love

Sweet Vale of Avoca how calm could I rest
In your bosom of shade with the friends I love best
Where the storms that we feel in this cold world should cease
And our hearts like the waters be mingled in peace

"The celebrated Irish poet Thomas Moore, who was born in Aungier Street, Dublin in 1779, wrote this beautiful poem, setting the words to a very old air called 'The Old Head Of Denis', which I believe was collected from the singing of Biddy Monaghan in County Sligo in 1837. The song is about the meeting of two rivers, the Avonmore and the Avonbeg, in the vale of Avoca near where Moore had stayed with friends. He was so taken with the beauty of the scene in Wicklow that he wrote the poem. I can remember it from very early on when it was learned at school or sometimes sung when friends or relatives had to stand up and perform a piece at a family gathering. The words are so beautiful and convey such a lovely sense of peace."

CAOLSHÁILE, RUADH – IRELAND'S ONLY FJORD

FROM THE BOAT HOUSE – ROSS CASTLE, CO. GALWAY

FAR FROM HOME

In 1996 there was a dramatic turning point in Ireland. Until then Ireland had been a country blighted by 'migration', which meant that more people left the country than came in. The population declined from about eight million people in the 1840s to about two and half million people in the 1960s, when I was born. There was a terrible potato famine in the 1840s, when over a million poor souls died, and another million or more left on the crowded famine ships, to escape starvation at home. After that there were waves of mass emigration, from the 1870s to around 1926 and then again it continued in the post-war period through the 1950s and 60s.

This outpouring of our people more or less continued well into the 1990s, when there was an estimated three million Irish citizens living abroad. Over a million of those were born in Ireland with most of them living in America and the UK. These cold figures hide the pain and suffering that this loss had caused in the towns, villages and communities of our country. Everybody lost someone they loved. It is hardly surprising then that the overriding theme of so many of our songs is the pain and loss of leaving home, losing loved ones or missing the places and people the emigrant had been forced to leave behind.

As I sing these songs, in far away places like Sydney or New York, I sometimes meet people who left maybe 50 years ago but who still talk of Ireland as 'home'. Sometimes the lyrics of the songs seem to view Ireland through sentimental, romantic 'green tinted' spectacles, a country that would now be unrecognisable to those who had left. But the imagery of the songs also expresses hurt feelings and painful memories that were sincerely heartfelt and experienced. Having had members of my own family have to leave to find work, I can relate to these songs and when I sing them all over the world my audiences relate to them too. Thank God that at last our young talented people are no longer forced to leave their homeland, and that so many who did go are now coming back home.

COME BACK PADDY REILLY TO BALLYJAMESDUFF

Percy French

The Garden of Eden has vanished, they say
But I know the lie of it still
Just turn to the left at the bridge of Finea
And stop when halfway to Cootehill
It's there you will find it
I know sure enough
For fortune has come to my call
The grass it grows green around Ballyjamesduff
And the blue sky is over it all

And tones that are tender and tones that are rough
Are whispering over the sea
'Come back, Paddy Reilly to Ballyjamesduff
Come home, Paddy Reilly, to me'

My mother once told me that when I was born
The day that I first saw the light
I looked down the street on that very first morn
And gave a great crow of delight
Now most newborn babies appear in a huff
And start with a sorrowful squall
But I knew I was born in Ballyjamesduff
And that's why I smiled at them all

The baby's a man, now he's toil-worn and tough
Still, whispers come over the sea
'Come back, Paddy Reilly to Ballyjamesduff
Come home, Paddy Reilly, to me
Come home, Paddy Reilly, to me'

"I have mentioned earlier how much I love the songs of Percy French and particularly the tongue-in-cheek humour he conveys in his songs. William Percy French (1854-1920) was born at Cloonyquin, County Roscommon, Ireland. His first attempt at song writing was when he was a student at Trinity College Dublin, where he trained as an engineer, going on to work for the authorities in County Cavan, as an 'inspector of drains'. He wrote his best songs during that period. He then became a journalist and later turned full-time to writing, painting and being an entertainer. He died of pneumonia in 1920 in Formby in Lancashire, where he had settled and he is buried in the local churchyard. He was such a brilliant songwriter that he boasted that he could write a song about any place or name and I understand that in conversation in a pub he was challenged by a jarvey called Paddy Reilly to write a song about the place where the man had come from. The result was this fantastic song, which I enjoy singing so much. What I think is really wonderful about this song is the way that French manages to combine his sense of humour with the sadness of missing a place faraway and yearning for happier past times. It is so beautiful and that is why it has survived so long."

A 'NEW IRELAND' SHOPPER AT INISHANNON, CO. CORK

I'LL TAKE YOU HOME AGAIN, KATHLEEN

T. Westendorf

I'll take you home again, Kathleen
Across the ocean wild and wide
To where your heart has ever been
Since first you were my loving bride
The roses all have left your cheek
I've watched them fade away and die
Your voice is sad when e'er you speak
And tears bedim your loving eyes

Oh! I will take you back, Kathleen
To where your heart will feel no pain
And when the fields are fresh and green
I will take you to your home Kathleen

I know you love me, Kathleen, dear
Your heart was ever fond and true
I always feel when you are near
That life holds nothing, dear, but you
The smiles that once you gave to me
I scarcely ever see them now
Though many, many times I see
A darkening shadow on your brow

Oh! I will take you back, Kathleen
To where your heart will feel no pain
And when the fields are fresh and green
I'll take you to your home Kathleen

"This is often thought of as an Irish song as it always seems to be sung at weddings and parties, but in fact it is not. It was actually written in 1875 by a German named Thomas Westendorf, a music teacher in Plainfield, Illinois, where the song was first performed. He wrote it for his wife while she was away visiting her home town near New York. A year later it was one of the most popular songs in America. The universal sentiment of the lyric and the great melody have combined to make it a classic popular song, sung by everyone from Bing Crosby to Elvis Presley and Johnny Cash – and in Ireland it became very popular when sung by Joseph Locke. I really like it and as I have a sister called Kathleen it is great for me to sing."

A HAND BUILT DRYSTONE WALL, CO. CLARE

"One of the most popular songs in America... a classic popular song, sung by everyone from Bing Crosby to Elvis Presley and Johnny Cash"

LOUGH MELVYN'S ROCKY SHORE

J. Farry

Lying in my bedroom in a London Hotel
Thinking about my folks at home I hope that they are all well
Thinking about my home town that I left when I was young
Thinking about the place I love, the village Garrison

Born and raised in Garrison on a little country farm
I grew up right near this town the place that I call home
London was the only place to make a few quick bob
So I left my home at 21 to find a decent job

But I'm going back to Ireland in the morning
I'm coming home to Garrison once more
And I'll wander through the village by the lakeside
I'm going to walk Lough Melvyn's rocky shore

Well I miss the friendly faces and the lovely country sounds
To see a place so beautiful you would travel far and wide
But I can't stand to be away from Lough Melvyn's lovely shore
So I'm coming home to Garrison the village I adore

But I'm going back to Ireland in the morning
I'm coming home to Garrison once more
And I'll wander through the village by the lakeside
I'm going to walk Lough Melvyn's rocky shore
Yes I'm going home to Garrison once more

"This is another really good song I perform by John Farry. He comes from the town of Garrison on the border in County Fermanagh very near the Sligo Mountains. So many young men in the 1950s and '60s went to London to find work on building sites and the construction of new Underground tube lines and when they had time off they would go to the Irish dance halls in the Holloway Road and on Kilburn High Road, like the National, the Gresham, or the Galtymore. This song would have been sung in Irish ballrooms in England and also in Ireland and I have been singing it ever since I performed in those places. In the summer of 1985 I did it in my show at an Irish Festival in London when Mick Clerkin saw me and then signed me to his record label. Around the same time, Mick McDonagh who was working for the label, remembers seeing me for the first time performing the song at another long-gone Irish venue called 'The Thatch'. It is another of those great songs for raising the pace of the show but has lyrics that have real meaning."

GARRISON, CO. FERMANAGH

AN EXILE'S DREAM

M. Graham

Come listen to the story of an exile so forlorn
Who's here today, so far away from the land where I was born
But still I smell the heather; oh I see her lakes so grand
For every night it's my delight to dream of my homeland

I can see the homes of Donegal, the hills of Glen Swilly
I see the moon behind the hill, the cottage by the lee
I can see my mother's homestead from where the thatching
gleams
I'll reach out and touch them when they're in my exile's
dream

Every hill and valley every mountain stream
From the Boyne to the Shannon from the Lagan to the Lee
Ireland is my homeland, the likes I've never seen
It's my Irish home far o'er the foam that's in my exile's dream

Oh and now that I am returning to sweet Erin's fragrant
shores
My fortune made my passage paid my days away are o'er
And in a rustic cottage awaits my colleen Mary Ann
With lips I've missed and longed to kiss I'll take her by
the hand

And we'll see the homes of Donegal the hills of Glen Swilly
We'll see the moon behind the hill the cottage by the Lee
And we'll see my mother's homestead from where the
thatching gleams
I'll reach out and touch them, no more an exile's dream
I'll reach out and touch them, no more an exile's dream

"When I first heard this song by Michael Graham I was amazed as it sounded as if it had been written especially for me and for my concerts around the world. The chorus mentions the homes of Donegal and Glen Swilly, the Boyne and the Shannon and the River Lee, all places I love and places that I sing about in other songs. It is just a fantastic song that expresses everything about the sadness of emigration."

5000 MILES FROM SLIGO

Johnny McCauley

An old map I have found
So in thoughts I am bound
For old Ireland's green mountains and streams
To the land of my heart through the heart of my land
I am wondering tonight in my dreams

As I view Sligo Bay
And not so far away
There's Cluny and the girl I once knew
And my eyes start to fill
As I think of Lough Gill
In this map they have coloured in blue

Oh I'm 5000 miles away from Sligo
Wondering why I ever had to go
Oh I'm 5000 miles away from Sligo
Pretending I'm on my way back home

Tubbercurry is there and there's Ballisodare
Ballymote holds old memories for me
From the Ox mountain range to the coast line of Grange
There Roscommon to Leitrim you will see
So from Sligo and home

Once again I must roam
Back along the long Highway 83
And my memories are gold, in the sadness I fold
And return here to reality

Oh I'm 5000 miles away from Sligo
Wondering why I ever had to go
Oh I'm 5000 miles away from Sligo
Pretending I'm on my way back home
Pretending I'm on my way back home

"When I started recording I chose this song to go on my first album. It is another of the really excellent songs by Johnny McCauley and was an essential part of my set when I started on the road. At the beginning, when I was not playing concert halls but was mainly touring dance halls, ballrooms and some Irish cabaret venues, it was important to have songs that the audience could dance to and this was one of them. I still do it now as I like the imagery that uses the names of places from the county next door to Donegal."

A PUB IN SLIGO

SUNSET ON SLIGO BAY

IT'S A LONG WAY TO TIPPERARY

J. Judge

It's a long way to Tipperary
It's a long way to go
It's a long way to Tipperary
To the sweetest gal I know
Goodbye Piccadilly
Farewell Leicester Square
It's a long way to Tipperary
But my heart lies there

Up to mighty London came an Irishman one day
As the streets are paved with gold, sure everyone was gay
Singing songs of Piccadilly, Strand and Leicester Square
'Til Paddy got excited, then he shouted to them there

Chorus
It's a long way to Tipperary
It's a long way to go
It's a long way to Tipperary
To the sweetest gal I know
Farewell to Piccadilly
So long Leicester Square
It's a long way to Tipperary
But my heart lies there

Paddy wrote a letter to his Irish Molly O
Saying, 'Should you not receive it
Write and let me know.
If I make mistakes in spelling, Molly dear,' said he
'Remember it's the pen that's bad
Don't lay the blame on me'

Repeat chorus

Molly wrote a neat reply to Irish Paddy O
Saying 'Mike Mahoney wants to marry me, and so
Leave the Strand and Piccadilly, or you'll be to blame
For love has fairly drove me silly, hoping you're the same!'

Repeat chorus

"This song is known the world over. It was not written by an Irishman at all but by an Englishman called Jack Judge. He was an entertainer playing the London music halls. He wrote the song a few years before the First World War and it was taken up by the 7th Battalion of the Connaught Rangers, a regiment in the British Army, comprising mainly Irishmen who had connections with Tipperary Town. When war broke out in 1914 they marched to the tune into the battlefields of France. It was taken up by other soldiers and then became hugely popular with the public. Of almost 200,000 brave Irishmen in the British Army almost 50,000 of them died. For a small country, that is an incredible loss. The tragedy was marked by our President Mary McAleese in 1998, when, in Flanders Fields, she opened the Island of Ireland Peace

Park, featuring a round tower built of Irish stone as a symbol of conciliation. The ceremony took place in the presence of Her Majesty Queen Elizabeth II and King Albert II of Belgium, all paying their respects to the brave Irishmen. On a less serious note, some people think that the soldiers had a second meaning for the word 'Tipperary' in the song, it being a euphemism for – how shall I put this? – A place of creature comforts! I wouldn't know. All I know is that it is a rousing song to perform in my Irish medley and everybody can sing along."

THE OLD BOG ROAD

O'Farrelley Brayton

My feet are here on Broadway
This blessed harvest morn
But oh! The ache that's in them
For the spot where I was born
My weary hands are blistered
From toil in cold and heat!
But oh! To swing a scythe today
Through fields of Irish wheat
Had I the chance to wander back
Or to own a king's abode
And oh! To see a hawthorn tree
Down the Old Bog Road

My mother died last springtime
When Ireland's fields were green
The neighbours said her wake
It was the finest ever seen
There were snowdrops and primroses
Piled up beside her bed
And Ferns Church was crowded
When her funeral Mass was said
But here was I on Broadway
A-building bricks per load
As they carried out her coffin
Down the Old Bog Road

Now life's a weary puzzle
Past finding out by man
I'll take the day for what it's worth
And do the best I can
Since no one cares a rush for me
What need I to make a moan?
I'll go my way and draw my pay
And smoke my pipe alone
Each human heart must know it's grief
Though bitter be the load
So God be with you, Ireland
And the Old Bog Road
So God be with you, Ireland
And the Old Bog Road

"What a classic emigration song this is – a very sad tale of a young man living in New York and mourning the death of his mother in Ireland from thousands of miles away. It was written at a time when it was not possible to jump on a plane and be back across the world in a few hours. In those days travel was by boat which was expensive. Many who left never got the opportunity to go home even for something as special as the death of a mother. The song has become a standard for anybody who sings Irish repertoire and has been sung by most of the famous Irish singers and also by others such as country star Hank Locklin. It was written by Teresa Brayton who was born in Kilbrook, Kilcock in 1868. In 1908 she herself emigrated to America to work as a teacher and continued to publish articles and poetry and later she became involved in supporting the cause of Irish Nationalism after the rising of 1916. Returning to live in Ireland in 1932, she died when she was 63 at her original home in Kilbrook. Eamon de Valera, the Irish president at the time, unveiled a memorial at her graveside in 1959. I could surmise that de Valera himself could relate to this song, as he had spent time in exile in America but his heart always lay in Ireland. I just think it is a classic song which is a privilege to sing."

THE CHAPEL AT ROSS CASTLE, CO. GALWAY

A REMOTE ROAD IN CONNEMARA

DRAMATIC COASTS

Being an island on the edge of Europe, we are so fortunate to have about 3,000 miles of beautiful, dramatic coastline. There is nowhere in the country that is more than about 60 miles away from the sea, but more than half of the population live, like me, within 10 miles of it. This means that we have a fantastic 'playground' of unspoilt beaches on our doorstep, as well some of the most stunning cliffs and breathtaking views to enjoy. Nothing can be more memorable or bracing than to wander along a deserted beach, with the sea birds flying overhead, watching the power of the sea, then to return to a feast of fresh crab claws or mussels at home or at a seaside pub. People often fly away for exotic foreign holidays, forgetting that we have so many treasures at home. Some of these fantastic coastal scenes have inspired marvellous songs.

WALKING THE DOG – FETHARD, CO. WEXFORD

GALWAY BAY

Arthur Colohan

If you ever go across the sea to Ireland
Be it only at the closing of your days
You can sit and watch the moon rise over Claddagh
And see the sun go down on Galway Bay

Just to see again the ripple of the trout-stream
The women in the meadows making hay
For to sit beside at her fire in a cabin
And watch the bare-foot gossoons at their play

Oh the breeze is blowing o'er the sea from Ireland
Are perfumed by the heather as they blow
And the women in the uplands digging praties
Speak a language that the strangers do not know

Oh, the strangers came and tried to teach us their ways
They scorned us for being what we are
But they might as well go chasing after moonbeams
Or light a penny candle from a star

And if there's going to be a life hereafter
As somehow I feel sure there's going to be
I will ask my God to let me make my heaven
In that dear land across the Irish Sea

"Is there anybody who has never heard this song or anybody who having heard it has not been tempted to visit the spot? The old city of Galway sits at the heart of a huge bay on the western coast of Ireland, with the Arran Isles out to sea. It is a really beautiful setting for the old town, which is full of interesting shops in narrow streets. The County of Galway, around the bay, has wild, remote and spectacular landscapes with some of the most dramatic coastlines in the county. There are several songs with Galway in the title, I have three of them in this book, but there are two with the same title, 'Galway Bay'. This one is the second, written by Dr Arthur Colohan in 1947. Although many singers have recorded the song, its international popularity probably comes from the highly successful version recorded by Bing Crosby. The song is just a timeless international standard which I enjoy performing."

THE CLIFFS OF DONEEN

Traditional

You may travel far far from your own native land
Far away o'er the mountains, far away o'er the foam
But of all the fine places that I've ever been
Sure there's none can compare with the cliffs of Doneen

Take a view o'er the mountains, fine sights you'll see there
You'll see the high rocky mountains o'er the west coast
of Clare
Oh the town of Kilkee and Kilrush can be seen
From the high rocky slopes round the cliffs of Doneen

It's a nice place to be on a fine summer's day
Watching all the wild flowers that ne'er do decay
Oh the hares and lofty pheasants are plain to be seen
Making homes for their young round the cliffs of Doneen

Fare thee well to Doneen, fare thee well for a while
And to all the kind people I'm leaving behind
To the streams and the meadows where late I have been
And the high rocky slopes round the cliffs of Doneen

"This is one of those songs that seems to have been around for ever and is known by us all. Christy Moore has a beautiful version of it and he says that he first heard it in 1965, when I was just a toddler. I can remember my sister doing a country version of the song and I also remember Irish Eurovision winner Dana, doing it too. Somehow I think that the song has a very simple theme but coupled with the lovely melody it works so well. Mind you, I think it is one of those songs that will confuse the dedicated tourist as I am not convinced that the cliffs described in the song actually exist. As the song says, the towns of 'Kilkee and Kilrush' can be seen so people seem to think the cliffs are in Clare, but Mick tried to find them and failed! He was told by a man in a pub that they don't exist and are just a feature invented with poetic licence for the song, but that may have been the drink talking! It is also possible that the cliffs are somewhere in north Kerry on the Shannon estuary near Ballylongford. There is a Doneen point above Ballybunion but from there I don't think you would be able to see the towns mentioned and even if there are cliffs in that area they must be very low. No matter, in spite of not finding the cliffs it is a lovely song and you could have fun trying to find them."

DINGLE BAY FROM THE IVERAGH PENINSULA

COULDN'T FIND THE CLIFFS OF DONEEN: THIS IS A BIT OF DINGLE BAY, CO. KERRY

HEAVEN AROUND GALWAY BAY

O'Shea

When they told me that Ireland was heaven
I said that's where I'm longing to stay
Then an emigrant voice said that's my land
If you please sir I'll show you the way

You will see smiling faces that greet you
With a cead mille a failte a stor
And a candle burns bright in the window
Of a cabin with only one door

When you see the moon rise over Claddagh
And the golden sun kisses the sea
Then you're on the right road sir, for heaven
For it's heaven around Galway Bay

In the church on the hill neath the moonlight
You can hear the sweet angel's voice sing
It's the angel whose heart I may gladden
When I give her my gold Claddagh ring

And the colleen who smiles so divinely
At the sound of the bell, stops to play
Just you turn and say 'God bless you' kindly
And to heaven she'll show you the way

An old-fashioned lady will greet you
Says 'Come in sir you're welcome to stay'
Then you are on the right road sir for heaven
For it's heaven around Galway Bay
Then you are on the right road sir
For it's heaven around Galway Bay

"This is another song about Galway Bay that I just love. When I filmed 'Peaceful Waters' in 1999, we included this song as I like it so much, even though Galway Bay was not on the Shannon Erne Waterway, the route of our journey at that time. If I get a break when I am playing in Galway, I love to take a walk from the hotel along the seashore on the edge of the bay and so often there are fantastic sunsets to be seen. The 'Claddagh' mentioned in the song was a very old fishing village of thatched cottages just outside the town; they became very run down and almost derelict. At a time when it was not fashionable to renovate property, they were demolished and replaced with some less than attractive modern houses. In doing so a little piece of the magic and history of the area were lost but the village is still famous for the 'Claddagh' ring worn as a token of love by both Irish men and women. I think this is such a good ballad and I like the pictures that the lyrics inspire. It always transports me back to Galway when I sing it."

A CLADDAGH RING

SUNSET ON GALWAY BAY FROM OUTSIDE LINNANE'S LOBSTER BAR – NEW QUAY, CO. CLARE

SONG FOR IRELAND

Phil Colclough & June Colclough

Walking all the day
Near tall towers where falcons build their nests
Silver winged they fly!
They know the call of freedom in their breasts
Saw Black Head against the sky
Where twisted rocks they run to the sea
Living on your western shore
Saw summer sunsets, asked for more
I stood by your Atlantic sea
And sang a song for Ireland

Talking all the day
With true friends who try to make you stay
Telling jokes and news
Singing songs to pass the night away
Watched the Galway salmon run
Like silver, dancing, darting in the sun.
Living on your western shore
Saw summer sunsets, asked for more
I stood by your Atlantic sea
And sang a song for Ireland

Drinking all the day
In old pubs where fiddlers love to play
Someone touched the bow
He played a reel which seemed so grand and gay
Stood on Dingle beach and cast
In wild foam we found Atlantic bass
Living on your western shore
Saw summer sunsets, asked for more
I stood by your Atlantic sea
And sang a song for Ireland

Dreaming in the night
I saw a land where no one had to fight
Waking in your dawn
I see you crying in the morning light
Lying where the falcons fly
They twist and turn all in your air blue sky.
Living on your western shore
I saw summer sunsets, asked for more,
I stood by your Atlantic sea
And I sang a song for Ireland

"In 1983, I formed my first group called Country Fever as I had left college by then to start my singing career. In the 1970s and early '80s, The Troubles in the North were not resolved and there were some sad and turbulent times for Ireland. The type of music I was doing was really what I am still doing now, but perhaps with more up-tempo numbers, to cater for the venues we were playing. Around that time there was, of course, a lot of other music about in Ireland. The pop music of the day was made by bands that had emerged out of the punk era and, apart from U2, the music was not really my cup of tea. There were also a lot of traditional Irish groups around and I liked some of them. When I was a student in Galway I had heard of one band from there called De Dannan, as they played in a pub called the Quays. So I pricked up my ears when one day in 1983, I heard a new De

FISHING BOATS – FETHARD ON THE BALLYTEIGE BAY

Dannan song being announced on the radio. It just stopped me in my tracks. The song was 'A Song For Ireland', sung by Mary Black with her wonderful voice. I thought it was one of the best songs I had ever heard about Ireland, with its message of hope for peace in the last verse and all the wonderful descriptions of the beauty of Ireland throughout the song. I was very moved. It had taken an English schoolteacher and his wife, Phil and June Colclough, to appreciate our wonderful country in such a way and to hope that peace would eventually come.

Little did I know then that Mick, whom I didn't meet until 1985, was the executive producer of the track and had recorded Mary Black in north London for the De Dannan album. I also didn't know that it would be more than ten years before the dream of the song came to pass. We now have our land of 'summer sunsets where no man has to fight'. If ever listening to a song could make you want to jump on a plane and come to visit Ireland then this is it. A fantastic song."

MYSTICAL IRELAND

Ireland is steeped in a rich history and one of the joys for visitors is to explore this ancestry and heritage, which can be found at our ancient historical sites, Monastic settlements, stone forts, countless castles and ruins and pre-historic places, such as the mystical Newgrange. Here, there is one of the oldest standing buildings in the world, built over 3,000 years before Christ. When the winter solstice comes around every December, a shaft of light shines through a special small hole in the roof over the entrance and passes along a narrow passage to light up the chamber inside. It is just an incredible structure and a magical place built all those years ago. Newgrange is just one of the places in Ireland of which legends are made.

ANCIENT STONE CIRCLE – BEAR

Our main culture and our language came with the arrival of the Celts about 700 years BC. Perhaps it was from the Celts that we got our gift of storytelling, as they left us many stories of warrior kings, fairies and heroes like Cuchulainn and Fionn Mac Cumhaill. After the Celts, Christianity arrived in Ireland around 4AD, giving us an incredible heritage and tradition that continues to this day. We now have so many churches and cathedrals and places of pilgrimage that reveal the deeply spiritual side of our country. We also have in Trinity College Library the beautiful illuminated Book of Kells, one of the oldest books in the world, hand crafted by the monks and something that must be seen to be believed.

DUNBRODY ABBEY, CO. W

From this time came the legend of the three leaf Shamrock, which St Patrick used to explain the trinity and which has been our national emblem ever since. Other stories and legends are just fun, like the myth of the Blarney Stone. They say if you kiss it you will never be stuck for a word. It's no surprise to know that Mick kissed it on 13 August 1963.

JLA

BLARNEY CASTLE

THE LABBY ROCK
CARRICGLASS, CO. SLIGO

GLENVEAGH CASTLE, CO. DONEGAL

THE OLD DUNGARVEN OAK

F. Hennessy

As I rode out one morning, going to Dungarven fair
I spied a pretty maiden with the sunlight in her hair
Her way was so delightful; her voice rang like a bell
And as I overtook her, I asked if she was well
Lay down your woollen shawl my love. I swear it is no joke
I'll tell to you the story, of the Old Dungarven Oak

As we approached Dungarven, the girl at me did stare
She asked me why I raised my hat, to a tree so old and bare
I told her of the legend, if the tree should e'er come down
There'd be a great disaster, and Dungarven would be drowned
Lay down your woollen shawl my love. I swear it is no joke
I'll tell to you the story, of the Old Dungarven Oak

And, then she started laughing, my face grew very red
She said that only fools believe, what those old legends said
Her laughter was contagious, now the truth to you I'll tell
By the time we reached the market place, I began to laugh
as well
Lay down your woollen shawl my love. I swear it is no joke
I'll tell to you the story, of the Old Dungarven Oak

As I sit here by my fireside, 'tis the autumn of my life
And the darling girl I met that day, she's now my darling wife
We have a lovely daughter, and a son to push our yoke
And it's all because I raised my hat to the Old Dungarven Oak
Lay down your woollen shawl my love. I swear it is no joke
I'll tell to you the story, of the Old Dungarven Oak

"Well, this is a legend full of mystery because if you go in search of the oak tree in Dungarven you will not find it. The song was written by a Welshman called Frank Hennessy who has connections with the Irish music scene. He originally wrote the song as 'The Old Carmarthen Oak' but it became the 'Old Dungarvan Oak' when recorded by Dermot Henry in 1972, reaching Number 5 in the charts. Frank lived in Ireland for a while and has written songs for many Irish singers. He now works as a radio presenter in Wales. I have been doing the song for a long time as it has a great rhythm to it and is a very popular toe-tapper in my shows."

DUNGARVEN HARBOUR

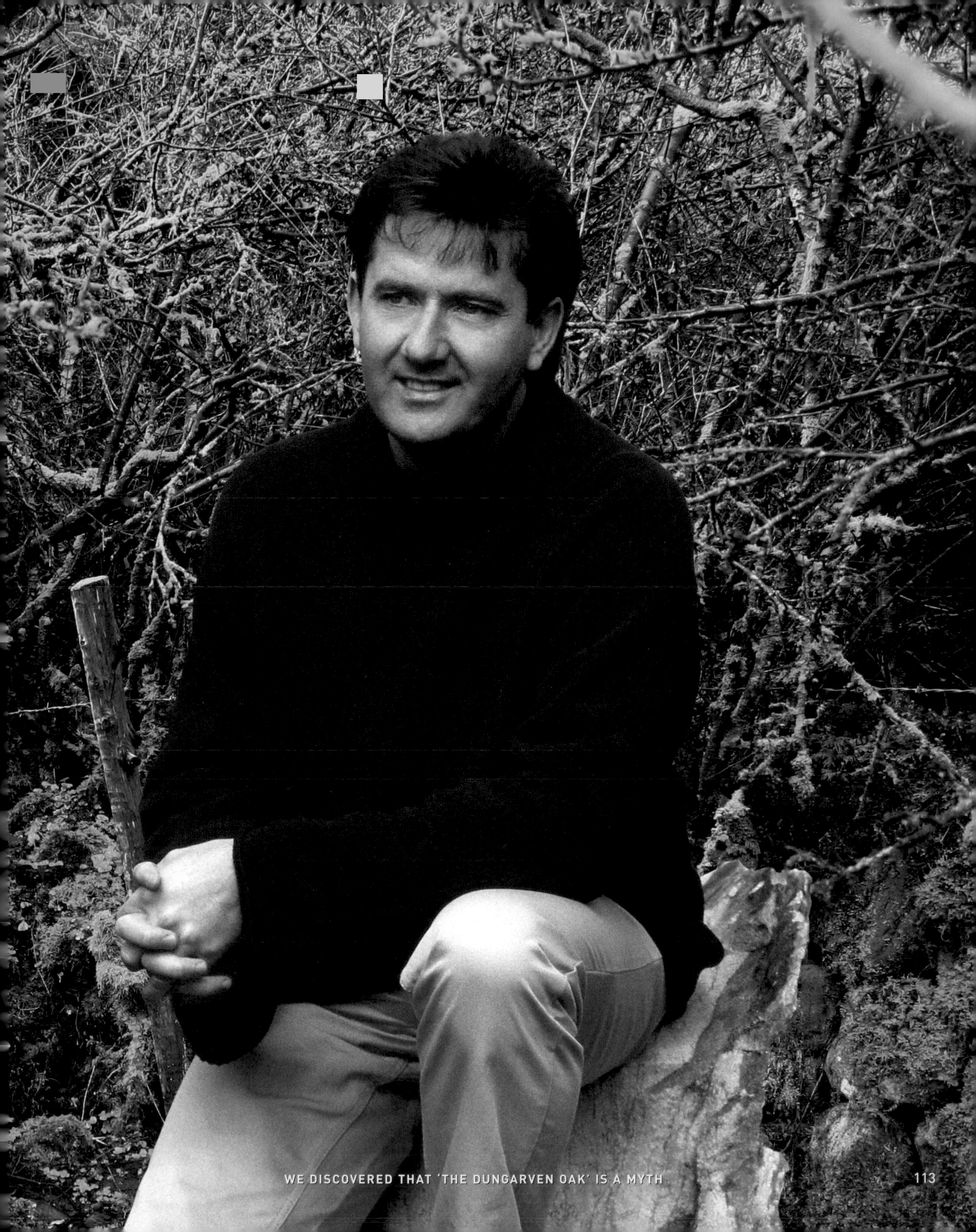

THREE LEAF SHAMROCK
Traditional

In the dark, a ship was anchored
On a bright St Patrick's Day
On the quay a lass was sighing
For her lover going away
In her hand she held an emblem
And it's parted leaves were three
And her parting words were 'darling
Look at these and think of me'

Three leaf shamrock I adore thee
Your three leaves I long to see
When there's brighter days in Ireland
I'll come home and marry thee

Just before the ship had started
As she'd laid her hand on mine
Just before that we had parted
She looked with loving eyes so kind
To my coat she pinned an emblem
And it's parted leaves were three
And her parting words were 'darling
Look at these and think of me'

But tonight I am an exile
Far from home, and far from thee
Next my heart I'll wear your token
Love no matter where I'll be
And although the seas divide us
And your face I might never see
When there's brighter days in Ireland
I'll come home and marry thee

Three leaf shamrock I adore thee
Your three leaves I long to see
When there's brighter days in Ireland
I'll come home and marry thee

"The Shamrock is the Irish National emblem, worn with pride on St Patrick's Day. Legend has it that Maewyn, a 16-year-old Welsh boy, was captured by Irish marauders on the rampage in Wales and was brought back to near slavery in Ireland. Working as a shepherd for the next six years, he eventually escaped, converted to Christianity, took up the name Patrick and spent some time studying in a monastery. To explain what the Trinity was, Patrick used the three-leaf clover, known as a shamrock, with three elements of one entity, to convert the pagan Irish and to illustrate the concept of Father, Son and Holy Spirit. He died on 17 March some time after AD 460 and before 493 and his followers started to wear the shamrock on the anniversary of his death. Ireland was converted to Christianity over the next 200 years and St Patrick's Day became our excuse for the party now celebrated all over the world.

In penal times all elements of Irish culture and language were banned, so the wearing of a small emblem like a shamrock became a badge of honour and pride. In this lovely ballad the significance of the shamrock is apparent as a token of love for the man who has to leave his loved one, but the song can perhaps be interpreted on a different level as an allegory for the struggle for national independence with the line 'when there are better days in Ireland I'll come home and marry thee'. I love the melody and the words and the sadness of the love story left with the promise of the man returning one day."

AWAY WITH THE FAIRIES IN THE POISON GLEN, CO. DONEGAL

FLOWERS OF IRELAND

For each year of my career a photo session has to be organised for my record and DVD covers. Apart from the sessions I have done in London, Paris or Tenerife, many of the sessions have been at home in Ireland and I have been lucky to have discovered so many beautiful gardens in different parts of the country. Some of these gems are hidden down the drives of private houses and some are set in the grounds of luxury hotels, but all of them are individual and special. The variety of the flowers and the settings are so beautiful and all are carefully maintained by dedicated gardeners to show them off at their best. Places like Powerscourt, Glenveagh, Birr Castle, Kilmokea, Mount Juliet, Russborough House, Mount Stewart and the National Botanic Gardens at Glasnevin in Dublin are all worth visiting. Many of the best flowers in Ireland, though, are the girls inspired by the songs.

ROSS CASTLE GARDEN, CO. GALWAY

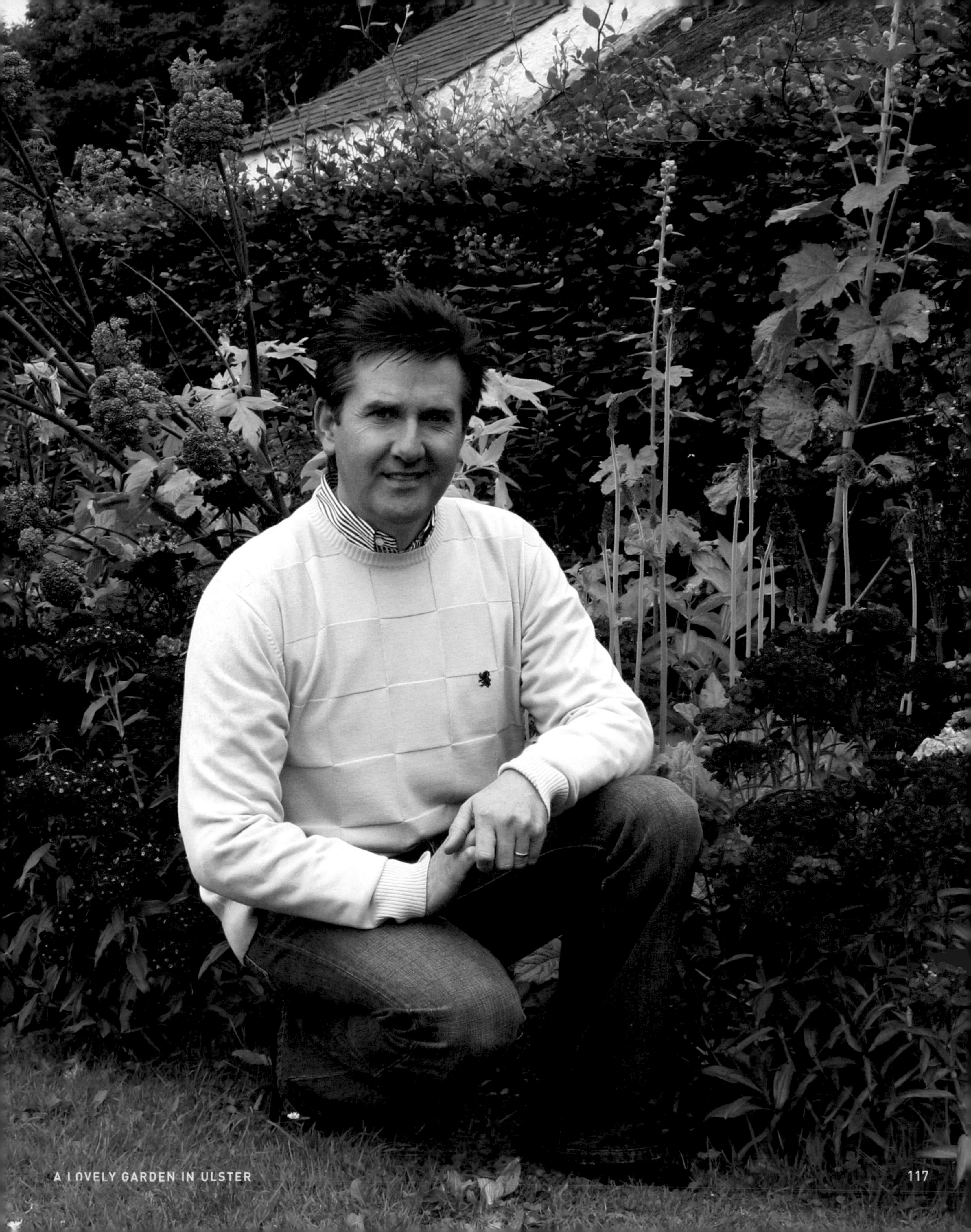

MY LOVELY ROSE OF CLARE

C. Ball

Oh my lovely rose of Clare
You're the sweetest girl I know
You're the queen of all the roses
Like the pretty flowers that grow
You are the sunshine of my life
So beautiful and fair
And I will always love you
My lovely rose of Clare

The sun it shone out like a jewel
On the lovely hills of Clare
When I strolled along with my sweet love
One evening at the fair
Her eyes they shone like silver streams
With her long long golden hair
I won the heart of a young sweet lass
My lovely rose of Clare

Oh my lovely rose of Clare
You're the sweetest girl I know
You're the queen of all the roses
Like the pretty flowers that grow
You are the sunshine of my life
So beautiful and fair
And I will always love you
My lovely rose of Clare

Now we walked down by the riverbanks
Where the lovely Shannon lies
And listened to the nightingale
Singing songs for you and I
And now to say goodbye farewell
To all you people there
For I have stolen the heart of one
My lovely rose of Clare

"When I heard this song for the first time I just loved it and recorded it almost immediately. It is just one of those songs that seems to capture the essence of Ireland: 'her eyes they shone like silver streams' or 'we walked down by the riverbanks, where the lovely Shannon lies, and listened to the nightingale singing songs for you and I'. It is so romantic and always takes me back to the summer time in the Irish countryside."

ROSS CASTLE COURTYARD, CO. GALWAY

A MOUNTAIN STREAM IN CO. KERRY

EILEEN McMANUS

Joseph M. Crofts & Leo Maguire

Last night as I lay on my pillow
A vision came into my view
Of a ship sailing over the ocean
And the wind so tremendously blew

On the deck stood a beautiful maiden
Whose features I'd ne'er seen before
She sobbed for the wrongs of her country
As she sailed from Erin's green shore

My name is Eileen McManus
My age it is scarcely eighteen
And I thank you, dear sir, for your kindness
For you don't know how lonely I've been

For the want of employment in Ireland
I was forced as an exile to roam
Far away from my home in Killarney
A place you all know well

It was then I awoke from my slumber
To look for my Eileen machree
It was only the face of my mother
With a fond smile stood gazing at me

Now the ship on the ocean has vanished
In fancy I see her no more
My beautiful Eileen McManus
The pride of old Erin's green shore
My beautiful Eileen McManus
The pride of old Erin's green shore

" 'Eileen McManus' is a song that I perform as a duet with Mary Duff. The tragic and perhaps mysterious lyric suits the two vocal parts and as I start the song on my own, it is always dramatic, when Mary makes her entrance. The song is an emotional ballad relating to emigration. Like many songs that have been handed down there are various versions and additional verses but this is the one we do. Sometimes it is known as 'Eileen McMahon' and maybe ours is more from that source. The song is set in the style of a Victorian parlour song and was written by Leo McGuire and Joseph Crofts. Eileen in the song comes from Killarney, which is a very beautiful part of the country in Kerry and in one of the verses that we do not include it mentions a 'spot' near Killarney called Aghadoe. This is the place where I was filmed for the 'Thoughts Of Home' video and album cover in 1989. Each year we always play a concert at the National Events Centre at the Gleneagle Hotel and I always look forward to it. How different Killarney must be now, with its fantastic hotels and restaurants, from the time poor Eileen had to leave. "

A CIRCUS ARRIVES FOR EASTER

AGHADOE, NEAR KILLARNEY WHERE I FILMED 'THOUGHTS OF HOME'   121

THE OLD RUSTIC BRIDGE BY THE MILL
Traditional

I'm thinking tonight of the old rustic bridge
That bends o'er the murmuring stream
'Twas there Maggie dear, with our hearts full of cheer
We strayed 'neath the moon's gentle beam

Beneath it a stream gently ripples
Around it the birds loved to thrill
Though now far away still my thoughts fondly stray
To the old rustic bridge by the mill

'Twas there I first met you, the light in your eyes
Awoke in my heart a sweet thrill
Though now far away, still my thoughts fondly stray
To the old rustic bridge by the mill

Beneath it a stream gently ripples
Around it the birds loved to thrill
Though now far away still my thoughts fondly stray
To the old rustic bridge by the mill
To the old rustic bridge by the mill

"Between Mallow and Fermoy in County Cork is a lovely village called Castletownroche by the river Awbeg in the Blackwater Valley. This is where H.P. Keenan, the composer of this Irish song, is buried. Nearby are the ruins of Bridgetown Abbey, a thirteenth-century Augustinian priory and also Anne's Grove, which has some lovely gardens that are open to the public. What is special about the village though is that at the old mill, which is currently being restored, there is a bridge which was the inspiration for the song. When the building works and the mill works are finished it will be used by craft workers. Quite a number of Irish singers have recorded this song – Louise Morrisey, Foster and Allen and many more, as it has become one of those classic Irish ballads. I recorded it for my very first album. It is a wistful song of unfulfilled romance from a man who longs for a sweetheart long since left behind."

OLD BRIDGE, CO. MAYO

NOREEN BAWN

Traditional

There's a glen in old Tir Conaill
There's a cottage in that glen
Where there dwelt an Irish colleen
Who inspired the hearts of men
She was gentle, hale and hearty
Shy and graceful as the fawn
And the neighbours loved that widow's
Happy, laughing Noreen Bawn

Then one day there came a letter
With her passage paid to go
To the land where the Missouri
And the Mississippi flows
So she said goodbye to Erin
And next morning at the dawn
That poor mother broken-hearted
Parted with her Noreen Bawn

Many years that widow waited
'Til one morning to her door
Slowly walked a graceful female
Costly were the clothes she wore
She said, 'Mother, don't you know me?
I've only got a cold'
But her cheeks were flushed and scarlet
And another tale they told

There's a graveyard in Tir Conaill
Where the flowers gently wave
There's a grey haired mother kneeling
O'er a cold and lonely grave
'Oh Noreen', she is sighing
'I've been lonely since you're gone
'Twas the curse of emigration
Left you here, my Noreen Bawn'

So you youths and tender maidens
Ponder well before you go
From your humble home in Erin
What's beyond you will never know
What's the use of gold and silver
When your health and strength are gone?
When you speak of emigration
Won't you think of Noreen Bawn
When you speak of emigration
Won't you think of Noreen Bawn

"This is a tragic emigration song with a difference, which is why I like it. This time the problem is dealt with from the perspective of a mother who has lost her daughter. There was a period some time ago after the famine years when so many people were still leaving the country that there was great concern among the clergy and politicians that Irish society would suffer forever if all the talented and strong people left. Many of those tempted to take a train or boat were encouraged to believe that staying at home was an act of patriotic duty and a number of anti-emigration poems emerged. Noreen Bawn was one of these. The poor widow in the song first suffers the loss of her daughter, who emigrates, but when she later returns in fine clothes it transpires that she is terminally ill so the widow suffers a second loss when her daughter dies. There is a warning in the song to suggest that going away in search of riches can have dire consequences and carries a risk of death. It has a different twist to the usual emigration song as well as being a lovely melody and that's why I am fond of it, recording it for my first album."

COTTAGE NEAR GLEANN, CO. GALWAY

"There is a
warning in
the song to
suggest that
going away
in search of
riches can
have dire
consequences..."

MAGGIE

James Butterfield & George Johnson

I wandered today to the hills, Maggie
To watch the scene below
The creek and the creaking old mill, Maggie
As we used to, long, long ago

The green grove is gone from the hill, Maggie
Where first the daisies sprung
The creaking old mill is still, Maggie
Since you and I were young

Oh they say that I'm feeble with age, Maggie
My steps are much slower than then
My face is a well-written page, Maggie
And time alone was the pen

They say we have outlived our time Maggie
As day did a song that we've sung
But to me you're are as fair Maggie
When you and I were young

They say we have outlived our time Maggie
As day did a song that we've sung
But to me you're as fair Maggie
When you and I were young
When you and I were young

" 'Maggie' is a wonderful song that has been learned and handed down from one singer to another. There is some confusion about the origin of the song. Some people think it is Scottish and others that it is Irish. I mentioned earlier that around the time I was living in Galway there was an influential traditional group called De Danann who played in the area. The first singer with the group was Dolores Keene from Galway; then they found a talented young singer from Ennis, Maura O'Connell and she recorded an album with the band called The Star Spangled Molly. It was a sort of concept album with a theme based on their awakened interest in the heyday of Irish-American music in the 1920s. I think the best track was 'Maggie' sung by Maura. Her version is beautiful even though it was a little strange at that time for a woman to be singing a love song to 'Maggie'. For this reason the track could not get air play in London so Foster and Allen recorded it and had their second hit in England with the song. "

As for the origins of the song, it was originally a Victorian parlour song and the confusion arises mainly because Sean O'Casey adapted it for his play The Plough and the Stars at the Abbey Theatre and his version was called 'Nora'. The real origins, however, come from Canada, where a poem was written by George Johnson and a teacher from Toronto, for his fiancée Maggie Clarke. When they were courting, she became ill with TB and as Johnson waited for her to recover he walked on a hill overlooking a mill and was inspired to write this song for her. They married and moved to Cleveland, Ohio but his wife sadly died in 1865. His friend James Butterfield, an English music teacher, set it to music and published it in 1866. Having created such a beautiful, enduring song it became hugely popular at the turn of the century then went out of fashion until rediscovered by De Danann in the 1980s. Now it is heard everywhere and is regarded as a classic 'Irish' song."

THE ROSE OF MOONCOIN

Traditional

Oh how sweet is to roam by the sunny Suir's stream
And to hear the dove coo 'neath the morning sunbeam
Where the thrush and the robin their sweet notes entwine
On the banks of the Suir that flows down by Mooncoin

Flow on lovely river, flow gently along
By your waters so clear sounds the lark's merry song
By your green banks I'll wander where first I did join
With you lovely Molly, the rose of Mooncoin

Oh Molly dear Molly, it breaks my fond heart
To know that we too now forever must part
But I'll think of you Molly while the sun and moon shine
On the banks of the Suir that flows down by Mooncoin

Flow on lovely river, flow gently along
By your waters so clear sounds the lark's merry song
By your green banks I'll wander where first I did join
With you lovely Molly, the rose of Mooncoin
With you lovely Molly, the rose of Mooncoin

"The love of an older man for a younger woman inspired this song, written in the 1800s by a 56-year-old local schoolteacher and poet named Watt Murphy. He fell in love with the 20-year-old local girl called Elizabeth who had the pet name of Molly. For them age did not matter as they courted on the banks of the River Suir, reading and writing poetry together. Elizabeth's father, the local vicar, took a different view and sent his daughter away to England. The poor teacher was devastated and wrote the song as a testament to their love. As I mentioned before when talking about the 'Mary of Dungloe' song, parents had much more control those days over their adult children and often caused a great deal of hurt. Mooncoin is a small village in the south of County Kilkenny where Gaelic games are popular so it is fitting that 'The Rose Of Mooncoin' has been adopted by the Killkenny fans as their anthem. I sing it because it is a lovely nostalgic Irish love song."

A RIVER FROM THE COMERAGH MOUNTAINS, CO. WATERFORD

A COTTAGE IN MOONCOIN

DOWN BY THE SALLY GARDENS

W.B. Yeats

It was down by the Sally Gardens
My love and I did meet
She crossed the Sally Gardens
With little snow-white feet
She bid me take love easy
As the leaves grow on the tree
But I was young and foolish
And with her did not agree

In a field down by the river
My love and I did stand
And on my leaning shoulder
She laid her snow-white hand.
She bid me take life easy
As the grass grows on the weirs
But I was young and foolish
And now am full of tears

Down by the Sally Gardens
My love and I did meet
She crossed the Sally Gardens
With little snow-white feet
She bid me take love easy
As the leaves grow on the tree
But I was young and foolish
And with her did not agree

" 'Down By The Sally Gardens' is a beautiful ballad and many people have sung it but my favourite version is that of Moya Brennan from the group 'Clannad'. The musical Brennan family come from Gweedore, just a few miles from Kincasslagh. I believe it is a traditional Irish song, which can be sung in Irish or English. It was included by the poet William Butler Yeats in a book of poems in 1889. 'Sally' comes from the Irish word for 'willow', saileách. Yeats based his poem on parts of a song he remembered an old Irish woman singing in Ballisodare, County Sligo. In 1909 the words were set by Herbert Hughes to an Irish air and this song has now become one of our treasures. Moya does a fantastic version of the song that I really like. **"**

THE GARDEN AT ROSS CASTLE

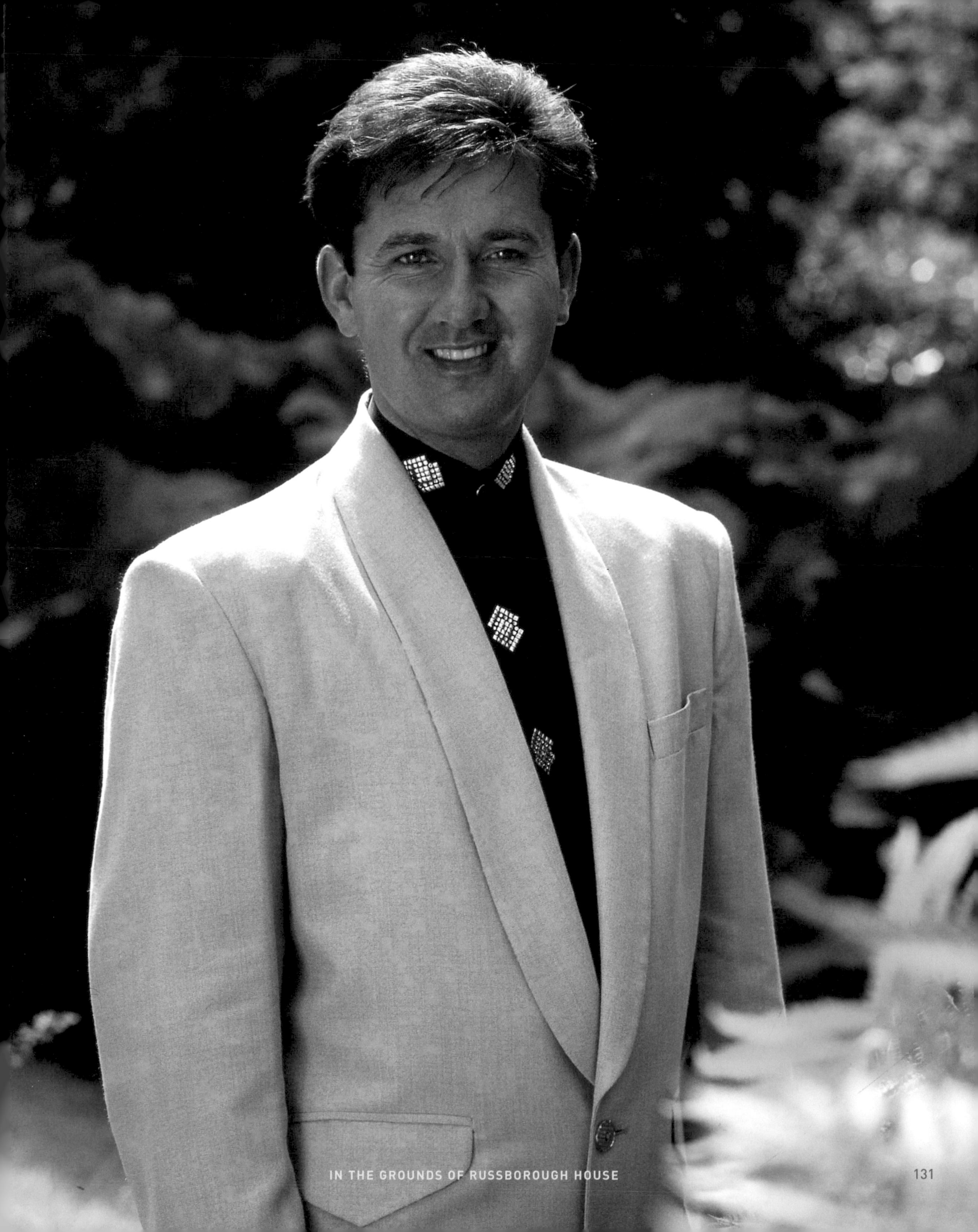

IN THE GROUNDS OF RUSSBOROUGH HOUSE

A BUNCH OF THYME

Traditional

Come all ye maidens young and fair
And you that are blooming in your prime
Always beware and keep your garden fair
Let no man steal away your thyme

For thyme it is a precious thing
And thyme brings all things to my mind
Thyme with all it's flavours, along with all it's joys
Thyme, brings all things to my mind

Once she had a bunch of thyme
She thought it never would decay
Then came a lusty sailor
Who chanced to pass my way
And stole her bunch of thyme away

The sailor gave to her a rose
A rose that never would decay
He gave it to her to keep her reminded
Of when he stole her thyme away

So come all you maidens young and fair
All you that are bloomin' in your prime
Always beware and keep your garden fair
Let no man steal away your thyme

For thyme it is a precious thing
And thyme brings all things to my mind
Thyme with all it's labour along with all it's joys
Thyme brings all things to an end

"This very old traditional folk song launched the career of singing duo Foster and Allen from the Irish midlands. Their version of the song was a Number 1 hit in Ireland at the end of 1978 but was then picked up by Ritz Records in England, who signed me later, and it became a big hit single. It shot Foster and Allen to fame and launched their international career, so they will always be associated with this song. In fact Christy Moore had recorded it in 1975 with a pure traditional version of the song. The history of the song goes back years. It was probably even known by William Shakespeare, as there is an historical reference as far back as the 1600s. The gentle lyrics of the song have a double meaning, which uses gardening imagery. The herb thyme represents virginity or chastity and the rose represents passion, so the song is a warning from a poor innocent country girl who has fallen for the charms of a 'lusty sailor' who 'stole my thyme away'. There are many versions of the song in England, Ireland and Scotland but after the Foster and Allen success we can claim it as our own. I like the old-fashioned style of the lyric and think it is a lovely song."

FISHING BOATS – KNIGHTSTOWN, CO. KERRY

NOT EXACTLY A BUNCH OF THYME, JUST A PROP MADE BY MICK FOR A PHOTO SESSION IN DONEGAL

THE ROSE OF TRALEE

C. Mordaunt Spencer & Charles William Glove

The pale moon was rising above the green mountain
The sun was declining beneath the blue sea
When I strayed with my love to the pure crystal fountain
That stands in beautiful vale of Tralee

She was lovely and fair as the rose of the summer
Yet, 'twas not her beauty alone that won me
Oh no! 'Twas the truth in her eye ever beaming
That made me love Mary, the rose of Tralee

The cool shades of evening their mantle were spreading
And Mary all smiling was listening to me
The moon through the valley her pale rays was shedding
When I won the heart of the rose of Tralee

Though lovely and fair as the rose of the summer
Yet, 'twas not her beauty alone that won me
Oh no! 'Twas the truth in her eye ever beaming
That made me love Mary, the rose of Tralee

"Of all the town festivals in Ireland, of which there are many, the Rose of Tralee Festival in Kerry is the best-known throughout the world and it is quite incredible that a local community could have been so far-seeing and innovative to create such a wonderful tourist attraction. Like many a good idea in my country the plan was devised in a pub over a few drinks. In 1958 a gang of local businessmen met Dan Nolan of the Kerryman paper in Harty's bar to come up with ideas of getting more tourists to the town when the races were on. Emigration had hit their local annual carnival event, which had faded, and they needed some new ideas. They took inspiration from the song and came up with the idea of an international festival or competition to find a winning girl who is most like Mary, the girl in the song – not just 'lovely and fair' but additionally ''twas not her beauty alone that won me, Oh no. 'Twas the truth in her eye ever beaming.' So the winning Rose had to come up to that standard as well as being a good role model for Ireland and throughout the world for the year of her reign. Contestants don't have to remove half their clothes and parade in bikinis in the Kerry weather for this competition; they are judged on their personality as well as their loveliness. At the end of every August since 1959 the town is besieged by beauties from all corners of Ireland and all corners of the world for the International final. There are Roses from Birmingham to Boston, Dublin to Darwin, Dubai to Denver, with France, London, Luxembourg, Newcastle, New York, New Orleans, New Zealand, Perth, Queensland, San Francisco, Southern California, South Australia, Sydney and Texas all represented. It is now a huge top-rating TV event with concerts and balls and all kinds of activities going on in the town. I have played there and it is always a great occasion.

The words of the song are credited to C. Mordaunt Spencer and the music to Charles William Glover who published the lyrics in 1845. However, this date belies a more romantic and festival friendly version of the songwriting. This is based on a nineteenth-century love story said to be set in song by William Mulchinock, a well-to-do Protestant merchant. Mary O'Connor was born in Brogue Lane in Tralee and was a poor Catholic girl living in a small thatched cabin with her family. When she was 17 she was offered work as a maid in William's mother's household and he fell in love with her. As with the Dungloe Mary, the relationship was discouraged because of their differing class and religion. William emigrated or, according to another account, he fled to India, as there was a warrant out for his arrest. Doubtless missing his lost love he returned six years later in 1849, when he felt that the coast was clear. On his return he stopped off for a drink at the Kings Arms on his way to find Mary. A funeral passed by and the barman told him it was for his Mary, a casualty of the potato famine. Heartbroken, he never got over it and it is alleged that he wrote the words of the song. Eventually he married and lived in New York but came back, living in Ashe Street until his death in 1864. His final request was to be buried next to Mary in the graveyard in Clogherbrien. No matter who did write the song, the story and the poem and the lyric make it a wonderful song to perform and it is known wherever I play."

OUR HOUSE IS A HOME

I am told that there are 70 million people in the world who say they have an Irish heritage. This astonishing figure is because from such a small island so many people had to leave and settle abroad. We Irish are very family focused and until recently very big families were the norm. It is no surprise, therefore, that the family home has a very great significance for us. The ideal of a home with a welcome on the mat and our mother always there with open arms is enshrined in our culture. Try going through an airport just before Christmas and it seems like the whole 70 million of the Diaspora are all trying to be back home for the holidays. I am no exception. I always return to Kincasslagh to celebrate Christmas with my family, and like so many other Irish people I have a very strong sense of loyalty and love for my family and our home. This strong emotion is reflected in so many songs that express the feelings we share towards our parents, loved ones and the welcome home, no matter if it is a small cabin, a farmhouse, a mansion or even a castle. Home is where the heart is.

A GREEN HOUSE IN CONG, CO. MAYO

MY IRISH COUNTRY HOME

John Farry

There's a place in Ireland I know well
Where I'd spend so many happy times
Where we'd sit for hours by the lakeside
With my dad's old fishing rod and line
And the warm summer evenings by the river
With my true love's hand clasped in mine
Where we made our promises together
That I'd be hers and she'd be mine

Oh take me back to those good old days
Those times not very long ago
Let me relive again those sweet memories
Of my life in my Irish country home

Now I'm far far away from my homeland
I'm living many miles across the sea
For I had to go abroad to get employment
Because at home there was no work for me
But I know I always will remember
Those golden days of home

And although I'm living o'er the water
My heart is in my Irish country home
Oh take me back to those good old days
Those times not very long ago
Let me relive again those sweet memories
Of my life in my Irish country home

Oh take me back to those good old days
Those times not very long ago
Let me relive again those sweet memories
Of my life in my Irish country home

"This is another great song from John Farry. It is also a song influenced by the emigration of the 1950s and 1960s. This song is very popular at the dances; it has the right tempo and a really good chorus that always has an appeal to audiences. It was especially so at the dance venues that we played in the early days in Scotland and England. The lyric would have been very appropriate and a recent image for these people at that time, as many would be from families that had left Ireland during those years. John has a great talent for catching the thoughts that Irish people may share.

I'm living many miles across the sea
For I had to go abroad to get employment
Because at home there was no work for me
But I know I always will remember
Those golden days of home.

It is a common shared experience transposed into a cheerful dance song which I still include in my shows."

AHAKISTA, CO. CORK

A COTTAGE NEAR LOUGH GILL, CO. SLIGO

GENTLE MOTHER

Traditional

By the side of the clear crystal fountain
There stands a lonely churchyard close by
There's a tombstone all covered with ivy
In remembrance of the one that's passed away

Shall I ne'er see you more gentle mother
In the fields where the wild flowers grow
I'm pining for a loss I'll ne'er recover
'Neath yon willow sleeps my gentle mother-oh

'Tis well I remember my childhood
When I toddled by my dear old mother's side
Picking flowers where they grew in the wildwood
When troubles and cares were not mine

Now some children love their mother with affection
There are more who break their mother's heart with pain
But some day they're sure to pay for their wrong doing
When crying will not bring her back again

"There was a very popular Irish singer who came on the scene when I was growing up. His name was Big Tom and he was a pioneer of the country's Irish sound that became very popular in the late 1960s and early '70s. Big Tom with the Mainliners really defined that genre of music from the beginning. In 1966 Big Tom (McBride) had a huge hit with this song 'Gentle Mother'. Perhaps because from the age of six, after my father died and I was brought up by my mother, the fact that this song was played on the radio all the time had a special relevance for me. It is a beautiful song that expresses our feelings about the most important person in our lives."

SPRING DAFFODILS

"Perhaps because from the age of six, after my father died and I was brought up by my mother, the fact that this song was played on the radio all the time had a special relevance for me."

HOME IS WHERE THE HEART IS

John Farry

As the raindrops are falling
I can hear your voice calling
Calling me back once again
I've been away for too long
But now I'm coming home
Back to your loving arms again

I miss the countryside so fair
And the good folk that live there
I've missed your tender kisses and your smile
Now I'm not too far away
I'm coming home today
And soon my feet will touch my native soil

And we'll do all the old things that we've always done
Dancing, romancing, together as one
Home is where the heart is and my heart's with you
No matter where I travel I'm coming home to you

The taxi cab is waiting
As I stepped out off the plane
'Cos I can't wait to catch the morning train
For now I'm returning
Where the home fire's always burning
To the one I love who's waiting there for me

And we'll do all the old things that we've always done
Dancing, romancing, together as one
Home is where the heart is and my heart's with you
No matter where I travel I'm coming home to you
Home is where the heart is and my heart's with you
No matter where I travel I'm coming home to you

"This song was written for me and recorded in 1984 very early on in my career and again it was one of the songs by John Farry that was good for the type of gig we were doing before I was able to move into concert venues. In the set in those days we had to keep a waltz dance tempo for a good proportion of the evening, as many people would come to dance. In fact, in the very early days half of them would not have had a clue who I was. John Farry himself had played all these venues with his own bands so he knew the scene well and his songs were dead on for what we were doing and invaluable for me in those early days. I still sing them, but now in seated concerts I am able to balance the show more and to be able to include many more of the classic ballads, as well as new songs."

MAIN PHOTO: THE KENNEDY HOMESTEAD, BIRTH PLACE OF JFK'S GREAT GRANDFATHER.   TOP L-R: COTTAGE, CO. SLIGO.   FILMING FOR MY   143
PBS SPECIAL AT A COTTAGE IN THE ULSTER FOLK MUSEUM.   COTTAGE IN KERRY.   BOTTOM: PATRICK PEARSE'S COTTAGE IN CO. GALWAY

MY SIDE OF THE ROAD

Sean McBride

Walking with my children in the good old countryside
Sharing all my time with them fills me up with pride
Teaching them the good life makes me full of joy
The way my daddy taught me back when I was a boy

That was so long ago but in my memory still
When I think about the old folks it gives my heart a thrill
There was never any money just the good old loving ways
Now the place that I was raised in is where I'll always stay

Some people like to travel far across the foam
But I'll always be contented just to stay at home
If you travel there's big money or so I have been told
But I think the grass is greener on my side of the road

I love to see grand children around this old homestead
If the good lord he will spare me to see my children wed
So I hope you'll show your young ones the love I showed to you
Then I'll die with peace of mind and let the old turn into new

Some people like to travel far across the foam
But I'll always be contented just to stay at home
If you travel there's big money or so I have been told
But I think the grass is greener on my side of the road
Yes I think the grass is greener on my side of the road

"What I think is interesting about this song and what attracted me to it was the sentiment expressed in the song: 'some people like to travel far across the foam but I'll always be contented just to stay at home'. I am a home boy and although I do 'cross the foam' quite a lot, nothing pleases me more than to be back home. There is more to the song than that though as it also expresses a feeling that the grass is not always greener on the other side of the road. So many people rush about chasing shadows seeking something they think is better, but if they stopped and recognised what they have they may be much happier. If you are blessed with good health and a loving family what more could you want? Every day I feel blessed for what I have and for what I have achieved and I am really happy on 'My Side Of The Road'."

A COTTAGE NEARBY

A LANE NEAR THE GAP OF DUNGLOE, CO. KERRY

OUR HOUSE IS A HOME

M. Sage

There's always a fire in the kitchen
There's always a kettle on the boil
There's no fancy carpets or no telephone
But the one thing our house is a home

A stranger is always welcome
Be at any time of night or day
So don't ever feel sad or lonesome
Just call as you pass on your way

There's always a fire in the kitchen
There's always a kettle on the boil
There's no fancy carpets or no telephone
But the one thing our house is a home

It's seen many happy and sad times
But it still remains through it all
Though times may have changed all around it
There's still a word of welcome in the hall

There's always a fire in the kitchen
There's always a kettle on the boil
There's no fancy carpets or no telephone
But the one thing our house is a home

There's no fancy carpets or no telephone
But the one thing our house is a home

"I recorded this song for my second album 'Two Sides Of Daniel O'Donnell' in 1985. It is such a great song, as it just says everything about the hospitality found in an Irish home: 'there's always a fire in the kitchen and always a kettle on the boil'. Since 1985 the economic changes in Ireland have been incredible and the standard of living has improved so much. Now there will almost certainly be fancy carpets and definitely a telephone, as well as a mobile or two and probably a microwave, since the prosperity from our 'Celtic Tiger' economy came, with all those makeover TV programmes that have us styling our houses. But I really hope that with this progress we don't lose the spirit of this song. That even if the hob now has flowers on it, the electric kettle or coffee maker will always be ready and that 'A stranger is always welcome' to our home. I will keep singing the song."

TRADITIONAL COTTAGE INTERIORS AT THE KERRY BOG VILLAGE, GLENBEIGH

SING ME AN OLD IRISH SONG

Brendan Graham

Sing me an old Irish song
Bring back the dreams that have gone
Sing me a love once so strong
Bring me the days when we were young
And true and I love you
And that old Irish song's
Calling me back to my home
Where once again you sing along
To an old Irish song

I see the mountains, the valleys
The green fields below me
I walked the highways, the byways
The old people show me
I hear the songbirds
Remember the soft words
We spoke after dark in the glen
I hear you calling me
Your songs recalling me
Back to those days again

Sing me an old Irish song
Bring back the dreams that have gone
Sing me a love once so strong
Bring me the days when we were young
And true and I love you
And that old Irish song's
Calling me back to my home
Where once again you sing along
To an old Irish song

I remember the old days
How I loved the old ways of living
There was more sharing, caring
More loving, more giving
How times have changed
Life's been all disarranged
Since summers we laughed in the rain
But I hear you calling me
Your songs recalling me
Back to those days again

Sing me an old Irish song
Bring back the dreams that have gone
Sing me a love once so strong
Bring me the days when we were young
And true and I love you
And that old Irish song
Calling me back to my home
Where once again you sing along
To an old Irish song

Sing me an old Irish song
Bring back the dreams that have gone
Sing me a love once so strong
Bring me the days when we were young
And true and I love you
And that old Irish song
Calling me back to my home
Where once again you sing along
To an old Irish song
Sing me an old Irish song
An old Irish song

A FARMYARD – CARRICKGLASS, CO. SLIGO

"I recorded this song in 1986 for the 'I Need You' album'. It was written by Brendan Graham, a very talented Irish songwriter who has recently had remarkable success with his inspirational song 'You Raise Me Up', which I have also recorded. 'Sing Me An Old Irish Song' is much more of a nostalgic song than 'You Raise Me Up' but I like the line in it 'that old Irish song calling me back to my home'. Brendan is a very good writer and in this song written in the style of an old waltz he conveys a gentle look back to times that were slower in pace with their traditional values, 'more sharing, caring, more loving and giving' or 'How times have changed, life's been all disarranged'. It is a soft hark back too for older people who have settled away to think back to lost youth and the more pastoral days back home when the family entertainment was not TV but an Irish song and a story around the fireside. It is a well-constructed song and I enjoy singing it."

FAR, FAR FROM HOME

John Farry

We'll say farewell tomorrow
And we'll leave you for a while
For our music it will take us on
Far far from this green isle
To sing in places we haven't been
And the ones that we well know
And we'll always meet the boys from home
Wherever we will go

Chorus
We'll be singing songs of Ireland to
The folks in Camden Town
When we play guitars in Boston bars
And friends will gather round
We'll be telling of the homeland
From where they have had to roam
When we get our sights on city sights
We will be far far from home

Now we are grateful for our culture
And we're grateful for the laughs
And we take them with us round the world
They are our arts and crafts
We know that all our emigrants
they are so proud to be
A part of all the songs we sing
Wherever we may be

Repeat chorus

We are happy with our music
Its what we love to do
And although we sometimes leave this land
We still return to you
We are proud that we can take afar
And leave with them a while
A part of this fair land of ours
We call the Emerald Isle.

Repeat chorus

When we get our sights on city sights
We will be far, far from home

"Those of us lucky enough to make a living as entertainers are fortunate that when we go away to work it is by choice in a privileged position. This emigration song is from the band's point of view and it very much reminds me of when I first began and toured in England. We were all packed in a van that I drove myself, often through the night to cities I was a stranger to. It was tough going and we were making no money but there were lots of laughs. What was always brilliant was the hospitality we were shown by the people from home now living abroad. It is really the same now, we travel in more comfort and we use planes to go further afield but we always meet friends and relations in different parts of the world.
I like to think that we take a little bit of Ireland with us to these places which is the message of this song."

DUNBRODY FAMINE SHIP, NEW ROSS

THE HOMES OF DONEGAL

Sean McBride

I've just called in to see you all; I'll only stay a while
I want to see how you're getting on, I want to see you smile
I'm happy to be back again, I greet you big and small
For there's no place else on earth just like the homes of
Donegal

I always see the happy faces, smiling at the door
The kettle swinging on the crook, as I step up the floor
And soon the taypot's fillin' up me cup that's far from small
For your hearts are like your mountains, in the homes of
Donegal

To see your homes at parting day of that I never tire
And hear the porridge bubblin' in a big pot on the fire
The lamp alight, the dresser bright, the big clock on the wall
O, a sight serene, celestial scene, in the homes of Donegal

I long to sit along with you and while away the night
With tales of yore and fairy lore, beside your fires so bright
And then to see prepared for me a shake-down by the wall
There's a home for weary wanderers, in the homes of Donegal

Outside the night winds shriek and howl, inside there's peace
and calm
A picture on the wall up there, our saviour with a lamp
The hope of wandering sheep like me and all who rise and fall
There's a touch of heavenly love around the homes of Donegal

A tramp I am and a tramp I've been, a tramp I'll always be
Me father tramped, me mother tramped, sure trampin's bred
in me
If some there are my ways disdain and won't have me at all
Sure I'll always find a welcome in the homes of Donegal

The time has come and I must go, I bid you all adieu,
The open highway calls me forth to do the things I do
And when I'm trampin' far away I'll hear your voices call
And please God I'll soon return again to the homes of Donegal

"This is just a fantastically evocative song with a wonderful melody that draws you back to the place that I love so much. The song says it all for me. 'For there's no place on earth just like the homes of Donegal.' I rest my case. The song was written by Sean McBride who, coincidentally, lived on Cruit Island near where we had our last home."

OUR OLD FAMILY HOME IN KINCASSLAGH

UNTIL THE NEXT TIME

These last pages are very special as I have included two songs that have great significance for me. One has always been part of my life, it is taken from the wonderful canon of Irish music, which as you will now have seen, provides me with a rich mine of treasures. The other is relatively new and is my attempt to put something back by my first attempts at co-writing a song myself. I feel honoured and privileged to be able to earn my living performing for audiences all over the world, doing exactly what I enjoy doing most and what I have always wanted to do, just singing these great songs. I am always very grateful for that opportunity and to all of you, the friends I have met on the road.

THE GROUNDS OF COOLCLOGHER MANOR – KILLARNEY, CO. KERRY

DANNY BOY

Frederic Edward Weatherly

O Danny Boy! the pipes, the pipes are calling,
From glen to glen and down the mountain side.
The summer's gone and all the flowers are dying
'Tis you, 'tis you must go and I must bide

But come you back when summer's in the meadow
Or when the valley's hushed and white with snow
'Tis I'll be here in sunshine or in shadow
O Danny Boy! O Danny Boy! I love you so

And if you come when all the flowers are dying
And I am dead as dead I well may be
You'll come and find the place where I am lying
You'll kneel and say an Ave there for me

And I shall hear, though soft you tread above me
And all o'er my grave will warmer, sweeter be
Then you kneel and tell me that you love me
Then I shall sleep in peace until you come to me

"Well if ever anyone had a signature song I think this one has to be mine. There are countless recordings of this amazing song and I have always treated it with great respect. Although there are over 100 different songs that can be sung to the beautiful haunting air it is the words of Frederic Edward Weatherly (1848-1929) an English lawyer that have made the song so very special and give it the mass appeal that it has. Surely it is one of the most recognizable melodies in the world and almost everybody can hum the tune. In 1910 Weatherly, who had never even been to Ireland, had already written the words to 'Danny Boy' when his sister-in-law in America sent him the tune we now know as the 'Londonderry Air'. She had heard some immigrant miners playing it in Colorado and it is thought to be based on a traditional air played by a number of harpists over the years. Weatherly found his words fitted like a glove and he published the song in 1913. What I think is nice is that Weatherly hoped that "Sinn Feiners and Ulstermen alike would sing his song". His wishes have come true for 'Danny Boy' has become a neutral symbol for all Ireland and all Irish people. 'Oh Danny Boy, the pipes, the pipes are calling'. The song is a legend, it is a symbol of our culture that gives both comfort and inspiration, raising emotions and our spirit. Being Daniel O'Donnell from Donegal it has to be my signature song and I am always proud to sing it."

A GLEN IN CO. DONEGAL

BY THE OLD BRIDGE – CRUIT ISLAND, CO. DONEGAL

UNTIL THE NEXT TIME

Daniel O'Donnell, Marc Roberts, Isla Grant

We came here together this evening
To meet with old friends that are true
'Cos over the years we've grown closer
That's what's happened between me and you

Somehow things in life keep on changing
And nothing it seems stays the same
But the times that we share
That old feeling's still there
And this song in my heart I declare

Chorus

May the road rise to meet you
And may all of your fears disappear
May all of your problems be small ones
'Til the next time we're all gathered here
Let's be thankful for all of the good things
We have in our lives everyday
So until the next time I see you
Close to my heart you will stay

Well now the time's come for the parting
Once more we must go our own way
Tonight we have made some more memories
And nothing can take them away

Leaving this place just remember
As we travel life's journey each day
The road that takes us away
Will take us back here some day
So until we're together this way

Repeat chorus

"Until the recent prosperity that has brought and kept people at home, Ireland has a long, sad tradition of saying goodbye. From the Famine years and even before, generations had to leave their homeland to find work in America, Australia or England. A saying often used when people were parting is 'May the road rise to meet you'. It is very Irish and I have always liked it, so I used the saying as the chorus when I wrote this song with Marc Roberts and Isla Grant. As I travel the world doing concerts I meet so many people but often only briefly for one night, as we always have to move on with the tour. It is so nice when we return to the same cities and we can all meet up again like old friends. The song is the title track of my last album and I think works well at the end of the shows to express how I feel."

NEAR DELPHI LODGE, CO. GALWAY

"Until the recent prosperity that has brought and kept people at home, Ireland has a long, sad tradition of saying goodbye."

This selection here has just been a taster of my favourite Irish songs, as there are so many to choose from. The choice of places is also just a little morsel. There are so many beautiful locations and scenes that it has been just impossible to fit more in. I hope however that with Mick McDonagh's pictures and his help putting the book together, that I have been able to give to you a flavour of my homeland. I also hope that from these pages you will have got an insight into what makes Ireland such a very special and unique place and why I love it so much. If you have never been to visit please do come, I promise you that you will enjoy it and of course there will always be a very warm welcome for you from the people of Ireland.

Cead Mille Failte.

Daniel
xx